Cordon Bleu

Salads

Cordon Bleu

Salads

SPHERE BOOKS LIMITED
30/32 Grays Inn Road, London, WC1X 8JL

First published in Great Britain in 1972 by
B.P.C. Publishing Ltd.

© B.P.C. Publishing Ltd., 1972

First Sphere edition 1973

Designed by Melvyn Kyte
Printed by Waterlow (Dunstable) Ltd.

ISBN 0 7221 2512 7

These recipes have been adapted from the Cordon Bleu Cookery Course
published by Purnell in association with the London Cordon Bleu Cookery
School
Principal : Rosemary Hume ; Co-Principal : Muriel Downes
Quantities given are for 4 servings.
Spoon measures are level unless otherwise stated.
Plain flour is used except where other types are specified.

Contents

Introduction

There are few edible plants that cannot be used in salads. This is one field of cooking where, equipped with a good basic dressing, even beginners can experiment to their hearts' content and have no fear of upsetting their guests.

There are however distinct national differences in the way salads are prepared. The French for the most part eat only one vegetable at a time, in a light oil and vinegar dressing. The English favour mixed salads, the most popular being lettuce, with tomatoes, cucumber and probably beetroot, most commonly dressed with some form of mayonnaise. The Americans are largely responsible for the refreshing introduction of fruit into an otherwise vegetable side salad. It is to the Americans, too, that we owe the introduction of mousses and jellies into the realm of salads.

Fresh vegetables are the richest and cheapest source of the numerous vitamins and minerals essential to our health.

With the modern definition of salads extended to include not only cooked and raw vegetables, fruit and herbs, but also meat, fish, eggs and cheese mixed with these, a salad can be a complete, balanced meal.

To make the most of salads, remember to buy only young and fresh vegetables. The older, tired specimens that are slightly cheaper will not look so attractive, will taste dull whether cooked or raw, and their nutritive value will not be as high. If you are cooking vegetables, take care not to overcook.

The other golden rule with salads is that the dressing should not be added until just before eating — otherwise the salad will go limp. If you are making a simple French dressing it is quite acceptable to prepare the dressing and toss the salad at the table in front of your guests.

We have packed the pages of this book of **Cordon Bleu Salads** with our favourite recipes from all over the world. But do not let invention rest here. There are dozens of unusual vegetables now on the market — the number increasing all the time as importing techniques improve. By experimenting with these, and by careful cooking and mixing of the more familiar varieties, you will be able to vary your menu as much as you like.

Rosemary Hume
Muriel Downes

Salads as starters

As a light starter, refreshing to the palate and not too filling, a vegetable, or vegetable and fruit, salad is delicious. This is the ideal time to be adventurous, and choose an unusual vegetable to serve on its own. Then you can really make a feature of it. If a rare vegetable is also expensive, you will not need as much for a starter as you would to accompany a main dish.

Particularly popular as starters are the salads based on fish or egg. These are slightly more substantial and are ideal if your main course is not going to be a heavy one.

If you wish to serve a selection of individual dishes as hors d'oeuvre, salads will be an obvious choice. Those we give from pages 11 to 19 will be a good start. The hors d'oeuvre course should consist of two or three 'straight' dishes — slices of salami, garlic or liver sausage, pickled herring or fillets of anchovy, together with several salads. In fact you go through the fish, meat and vegetable courses in miniature. The number of dishes served will depend on the number of guests, but for a party of six you can serve up to eight or ten.

The traditional hors d'oeuvre dish is rectangular, about two and a half inches deep and usually in white china. You can use any convenient dishes or buy a tray set fitted with curved dishes.

Presentation is worth a little extra thought for a first course - after all this is the first indication your guests have of the treats in store. If the first dish on the menu looks as well as tastes delicious, they will be well disposed to enjoy the rest. Given a little imagination, nothing pleases like the sight of a fresh salad dish, or cleanses the palate so well for the subtle dishes to follow.

Eggs mayonnaise

3-4 eggs (hard-boiled)
$\frac{1}{4}$ pint thick mayonnaise (using lemon juice instead of vinegar to sharpen it)
2 dessertspoons roughly chopped parsley
few prawns (shelled) — optional

A curry-flavoured mayonnaise, as used for the curried potato salad on page 18, may be substituted.

Method
Cut the eggs in half lengthways. Arrange in dish, rounded side up. Coat with the mayonnaise and sprinkle well with the parsley.

Prawns can be scattered over the eggs before coating them with the mayonnaise.

Watchpoint When coating eggs with mayonnaise make sure it is really thick, otherwise it will slide off the whites and spoil the appearance of the dish.

Russian or vegetable salad

1 large beetroot (cooked and diced)
1 carrot (diced)
2-3 tablespoons peas
1 potato (diced)
French dressing (to moisten)
2-3 tablespoons mayonnaise

Method
Put beetroot into a bowl. Cook carrot in pan of boiling water until barely tender, then add peas and cook for a further 2-3 minutes, or until both vegetables are tender. Drain and refresh.

Cook diced potato in boiling water until just tender (5-6 minutes). Drain it and add to the beetroot with the peas and carrot. Moisten with French dressing. Leave until all is cold, then stir in 2-3 tablespoons thick mayonnaise.

Watchpoint The combined amount of carrot, peas and potato should be half that of the beetroot.

Note : serve a selection of the salads given on pages 11-19 together as hors d'oeuvre. If you wish to serve any of these dishes singly, you will need to increase the quantity.

Recipes for salad dressings (eg. French dressing and mayonnaise) and **flavoured vinegars** are given on pages 128-134.

Herring and dill cucumber salad

2-3 herring fillets
1 Spanish onion (sliced)
2 dill cucumbers (sliced)
French dressing (made with dry
white wine instead of vinegar)

In many delicatessens herring fillets preserved in white wine may be bought quite cheaply. These, cut into strips diagonally and sprinkled with grated horseradish or mixed with horseradish cream, make an excellent hors d'oeuvre. Alternatively, these fillets may be made into a salad as in this recipe. They weigh about 4 oz each and are sold by the fillet rather than by the weight.

Method

Cut fillets into strips diagonally. Set aside. Push onion slices out into rings. Blanch for 5-6 minutes, then drain and refresh.

Arrange herring fillets in centre of serving dish, surround with the cucumber and place the onion round that. Spoon over enough French dressing to moisten well.

Herring and dill cucumber salad with onion rings and French dressing

Anchovy and bean salad

2-3 oz haricot, or butter, beans (well
   soaked and simmered until tender),
   or 1 can butter beans (drained
   from their liquid)
1 small can anchovy fillets

For dressing
$\frac{1}{2}$ teaspoon grated onion
$\frac{1}{2}$ tablespoon white wine
   vinegar
2 tablespoons oil
1 teaspoon anchovy essence
2 tablespoons double cream
1 dessertspoon chopped parsley

Method
Combine all ingredients for the
dressing, mix with the beans.
Put salad in serving dish. Have
ready the anchovy fillets, split
in two lengthways. Arrange
these lattice-fashion over salad.

Anchovy and bean salad decorated lattice-fashion

Frankfurter and ham salad

1 pair of frankfurter sausages
$\frac{1}{4}$ lb ham (cooked and thinly sliced)
$\frac{1}{4}$ lb tomatoes
1 red, or green, pepper (shredded and blanched)

For dressing
1 tablespoon white wine vinegar
1 teaspoon tomato purée
3 tablespoons oil
salt and pepper
caster sugar (to taste)

Method
Poach the sausages in boiling water for 5-6 minutes; then drain and cool. Shred the ham. Scald, skin and quarter the tomatoes; flick out the seeds and cut away the stalk. Slice each quarter into three.

Slice sausages diagonally and put into a bowl with the ham, tomatoes and pepper. Combine the ingredients for the dressing, season to taste, mix well and fork lightly into the sausage mixture.

Frankfurter and ham salad, with pepper and tomatoes

Italian salad

2 oz pasta shells
$\frac{1}{4}$ lb ham (cooked and sliced)
2 oz black olives (halved and
   stoned)
2-3 tablespoons thick
   mayonnaise
1 teaspoon French mustard

Method
Simmer pasta shells in pan of boiling salted water for about 7 minutes or until just tender. Drain and refresh them.

Shred the ham and mix this with the olives and pasta. Add mustard to mayonnaise and stir enough into the salad to bind it together.

Italian salad (pasta shells, ham and olives) with mayonnaise

Rice, tomato and black olive salad

3 tablespoons rice
$\frac{1}{4}$ lb tomatoes (ripe and firm)
2 oz button mushrooms
2 oz black olives (halved and
   stoned)
2 tablespoons water
squeeze of lemon juice
2-3 tablespoons French dressing
   (made with dry white wine instead
   of vinegar)
salt and pepper

Method

Boil rice, drain, refresh and dry. Scald and skin tomatoes, quarter, and flick out seeds, then cut away the stalk. Cut each quarter in half lengthways.

Wash and trim mushrooms, quarter and cook for 2-3 minutes in the water with a good squeeze of lemon juice. Cook quickly, uncovered, so that liquid is well reduced by the time mushrooms are cooked ; shake and stir well.

Mix all ingredients with a fork, season well and moisten with French dressing.

Rice, tomato and black olive salad, with button mushrooms

Sweetcorn, pepper and pickled onion salad

1 large can sweetcorn kernels
salt and pepper
2 caps of canned pimiento
   (coarsely chopped)
1 tablespoon small pickled onions
   (quartered, or thinly sliced)
French, or lemon, dressing (as
   for tomato salad — see page 113)

Some brands of canned sweetcorn already contain sweet
pepper, in which case do not
add pimiento.

Method
Drain sweetcorn well from its
liquid; put it into a bowl,
season well and add the
pimiento and the onions.
Moisten sweetcorn mixture
with the chosen dressing and
turn into a serving dish.

Sweetcorn, pepper and pickled onion salad, with dressing

Curried potato salad

about ¾ lb small new potatoes,
  or 1 small can
French dressing (to coat
  potatoes)
scant ¼ pint thick mayonnaise

For curry mixture
1 shallot, or ½ small onion
  (sliced)
2 tablespoons olive oil
2 dessertspoons curry powder
1 teaspoon paprika pepper
½ cup of tomato juice, or
  2 teaspoons tomato purée
  mixed with ½ cup of water
1 slice of lemon
1 dessertspoon apricot jam, or
  redcurrant jelly

Method

To make curry mixture : soften shallot or onion in oil, then add the curry and paprika ; cook for 1 minute, then add tomato juice or purée, lemon, and jam or jelly. Cover, simmer for 7-10 minutes, then strain. Keep this mixture in a small jar or covered container until wanted.

Boil potatoes in their skins, then peel and toss them in French dressing while still hot. If using canned potatoes, drain them thoroughly and season with lemon juice, salt and pepper before adding French dressing. Add enough curry mixture to flavour the mayonnaise to taste. Put potatoes on a serving dish and coat with the mayonnaise.

Mushrooms Philippe

4-6 oz button mushrooms
1 large tablespoon olive oil
1 shallot (finely chopped)
1 wineglass red wine
1 teaspoon freshly chopped thyme
1-2 tablespoons French dressing
  (preferably made with red wine
  vinegar)
salt and pepper

Method

Wash and trim mushrooms (cut off stalks level with caps, slice stalks lengthways and put with mushroom caps).

Heat oil in a small frying pan, put in the mushrooms and the shallot. Fry briskly for about 3 minutes, turning and stirring them all the time.

Lift out mushroom mixture with a draining spoon into a bowl. Pour wine into the pan and boil until it is reduced by half. Add to the mushrooms with the herbs and French dressing. Season well, cover, and leave until cold.

Spiced onions

½-¾ lb button onions
½ lb ripe tomatoes
2 wineglasses white wine
3 tablespoons olive oil
salt and pepper
1 teaspoon finely chopped
   fennel
1 teaspoon coriander seeds

Method
Peel the onions very carefully,
blanch for 7 minutes, drain and
return to the pan. Skin the
tomatoes, squeeze out the
seeds, chop flesh roughly and
add to the pan with the wine,
oil, seasoning and spices. Cover
pan and simmer gently for 40
minutes, when onions should
be very tender but still whole.

Lift onions out carefully into
serving dish. Strain the liquid
over them and serve very cold.

Tunny fish and prawn salad

1 small head of celery
1 small can (approximately 7 oz)
   tunny fish
2-3 oz prawns (shelled)
French dressing (to moisten)
1 dessertspoon chopped parsley

Method
Cut celery stalks first into 1½-
inch lengths, then down into
sticks. Soak these in iced water
for 30 minutes, then drain and
dry thoroughly.

Drain oil from tunny fish and
break it into large flakes with a
fork. Add to the prawns with
the celery. Moisten well with
the French dressing and add
parsley.

Crab salad printanier

1 medium-size crab, or 8 oz crab
   meat (frozen, or canned)
4 globe artichokes, or canned
   artichoke hearts
2 tablespoons French dressing
rind and juice of 1 orange
2 oz black olives (stoned)
$\frac{1}{2}$ pint mayonnaise
4 large lettuce leaves

*Carefully removing the outer leaves
of the cooked artichoke ; the centre
leaves and the choke have already
been putted out and discarded*

Method

Trim the artichokes and cook them in boiling, salted water for 45 minutes or until a leaf can be pulled out easily. Drain and refresh them. Pull out the centre leaves carefully, scrape away the choke and then remove each leaf, one by one, and discard. Spoon the French dressing over the hearts and leave them to marinate until cold.

Remove a strip of orange rind with a potato peeler, cut it in fine shreds and cook for 2-3 minutes in boiling water until tender; then drain. Grate a little of the remaining orange rind.

Watchpoint The rind must be grated on the very finest side of the grater (nutmeg grater); make sure that only the zest is used and none of the pith.

Flavour the mayonnaise to taste with a little strained orange juice and the finely grated orange rind.

Arrange the lettuce leaves on individual salad plates, place an artichoke heart on top and cover with crab meat; spoon over the mayonnaise. Garnish with the shredded orange rind and olives, and serve with brown bread and butter.

Swedish roll mop salad

3-4 roll mop herrings
1 lb new potatoes
oil and vinegar dressing (made with 6 tablespoons olive oil and 2 tablespoons white wine vinegar)
1-2 dill cucumbers (sliced)
2 tablespoons freshly chopped dill

Method

Boil the new potatoes with the skins on. Peel them while hot, then quarter or slice them, according to size, and moisten with the dressing. Leave to cool.

Cut the roll mops into shreds; mix these and the cucumber slices with the potatoes, adding more dressing, if necessary, and the fresh dill. Pile salad in a dish for serving.

Rice, prawn and almond salad

1 large onion (finely chopped)
1 oz butter
4 oz shelled prawns
cooked long grain rice (allow 1 oz per person)
2 oz almonds (blanched and shredded)
¼ pint French dressing

Method

Cook the chopped onion in the butter until soft. Chop the prawns and mix with the rice. Add the prepared almonds and onion to the rice and stir in the French dressing. Serve salad in a large bowl.

Mussel salad

2 quarts mussels
1 onion (sliced)
1 carrot (sliced)
1 wineglass white wine
$\frac{1}{4}$ pint water
bouquet garni
6-8 peppercorns
$\frac{1}{4}$ pint chicken stock
4 oz rice
3 tablespoons oil
1 shallot (finely chopped)
$\frac{1}{2}$ bayleaf
1 head of celery
4 oz white mushrooms
juice of $\frac{1}{2}$ lemon
pepper (ground from mill)
4 tablespoons double cream
1 tablespoon chopped parsley

Method

Wash and scrub the mussels in several changes of water and place in a saucepan with the onion, carrot, wine, water, bouquet garni and peppercorns. Cover the pan and bring to the boil. Now shake the pan once or twice and simmer for 2-3 minutes, until all the mussel shells are open. Lift the mussels from the saucepan into a china bowl with a draining spoon and strain the liquid in the pan through muslin into another basin, measure and make up to $\frac{1}{2}$ pint with chicken stock.

Wash the rice and put in a pan with the oil and the shallot. Pour over the mussel liquor (mixed with stock) and bring to the boil, add bayleaf, cover the pan and cook until the rice is tender and the stock absorbed (about 18 minutes).

Meanwhile wash the celery and cut into sticks about 1 inch long. Wash and trim the mushrooms, cut them in thick slices and

Some of the raw ingredients for mussel salad, and the salad being mixed

leave to marinate in the lemon juice and pepper.

Take the mussels from their shells and remove the beards. Mix the mussels with the mushrooms and turn the rice into a bowl to cool. Drain and dry the celery. When the rice is quite cold, mix the celery, mussels and mushrooms into it with a fork, taste for seasoning and then add the cream. Pile into an entrée dish and dust with chopped parsley.

Eggs Connaught

6 hard-boiled eggs
$\frac{1}{4}$ pint milk
1 slice of onion
blade of mace
6 peppercorns
$3\frac{1}{2}$ oz butter
1 tablespoon flour
salt and pepper
1 packet Demi-Sel cheese
1 teaspoon paprika pepper
4 oz prawns (shelled)
$\frac{1}{2}$ bunch of watercress (to garnish)

Piping bag with $\frac{1}{2}$-inch plain nozzle (optional)

While rubbing yolks through a strainer, stop whites hardening by keeping in a bowl of cold water

Method

Scald the milk with the onion, mace and peppercorns, tip into a jug, cover and leave to infuse. Rinse the pan with cold water, drop in $\frac{1}{2}$ oz butter, heat gently and blend in the flour. Strain on the milk and add salt. Stir continuously, bring milk to the boil, cook 1 minute. Turn on to a plate, cover with buttered paper to prevent a skin forming and leave sauce until cold. Cream remaining butter until soft.

Cut the hard-boiled eggs in two lengthways, scoop out the yolks and rub through a wire strainer; keep the whites in a bowl of water as they soon get hard if exposed to air. Work the yolks with the butter, cheese, paprika and cold sauce. Chop half the prawns finely, add to the mixture and season to taste. Drain and dry the egg whites and have ready a round serving dish or use a cake platter.

Spoon a drop of filling on to the dish to hold each egg white in position, arrange them in a circle and then fill each with the mixture, or you can use a piping bag with a $\frac{1}{2}$ inch plain nozzle. Scatter over the remaining prawns (split in half, if large) and dust with paprika. Place the watercress in the middle and serve brown bread and butter separately.

For a very special party this recipe can be prepared with smoked salmon in place of prawns. Save a little smoked salmon to cut into fine shreds and scatter over.

Eggs mollets à l'indienne

5 eggs
4 oz long grain Patna rice (cooked, drained and dried)
2-3 tablespoons French dressing
$\frac{1}{2}$ pint thick mayonnaise
salt and pepper

To garnish
pimiento (shredded)
watercress

For curry mixture
1 shallot (finely chopped)
1 tablespoon oil
1 dessertspoon curry powder
1 teaspoon paprika pepper
1 teaspoon tomato purée (diluted with $\frac{1}{2}$ cup of water), or $\frac{1}{2}$ cup of tomato juice
2 slices of lemon
1 dessertspoon apricot jam

Method

First prepare the curry mixture : soften the shallot in oil, add curry powder and paprika and after 3-4 seconds the remaining ingredients. Stir well and simmer for 4-5 minutes. Strain and set mixture aside.

Softboil or poach the eggs. Moisten the rice with a little French dressing ; arrange down the centre of a serving dish.

Add enough of the curry mixture to the mayonnaise to flavour it well. Adjust seasoning and spoon curry mayonnaise over the eggs. Garnish with the pimiento and watercress.

A l'indienne means, literally, in Indian style. The term is usually applied to dishes that contain either curry or chutney, or both, accompanied by a dish of plain boiled rice.

Eggs mollet à l'indienne — in a curry mayonnaise, garnished with shredded pimiento and watercress

Eggs mimosa

4 **large eggs (hard-boiled)**
4-6 **oz shrimps, or prawns**
   (shelled and coarsely chopped)
½ **pint thick mayonnaise**
watercress (to garnish)

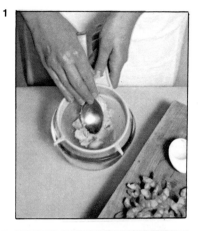

This is one of the best and simplest egg dishes for a first course. Serve with brown bread and butter.

Method

Cool eggs and peel. Cut them in half lengthways, scoop out yolks and carefully push half of them through a bowl strainer into a basin. Add the shrimps or prawns. Mix and bind with 1-2 tablespoons mayonnaise.

Wash whites, dry them and place on a serving dish. Fill with the prawn mixture. Thin the rest of the mayonnaise slightly with 1 tablespoon of hot water and coat the eggs with this.

Hold strainer over eggs and push the rest of the yolks through. Garnish dish with watercress.

1 For eggs mimosa, sieve half the yolks, mix with shrimps or prawns *2 Bind together with mayonnaise* *3 Fill egg whites with this mix-ture and sieve remaining yolks on top* *4 Garnish with watercress*

Eggs Mikado

6 eggs
4 oz long grain Patna rice
2 caps of canned pimiento
   (shredded)
2-3 sticks, or 1 small head, of celery
   (shredded)
2-3 tablespoons French dressing
$\frac{1}{4}$ pint thick mayonnaise
1 tablespoon chopped parsley
   mixed with pinch of chopped
   fresh herbs — optional
watercress (to garnish) — optional

The leftover white of the hard-boiled egg may be shredded and added to the rice with the pimiento and celery.

Method
Poach 5 of the eggs and keep in cold water until wanted. Hardboil the remaining egg.

Cook rice in plenty of boiling, salted water for about 10 minutes until tender; drain, rinse with hot water, then drain again and dry thoroughly.

Fork the prepared pimiento and celery into the rice (adding shredded white of the hard-boiled egg, if wished) and moisten with French dressing. Spoon this salad down the centre of a serving dish. Drain and dry poached eggs and set them on the rice.

Add 1 dessertspoon of hot water to the mayonnaise to thin it, if necessary, and use a little to coat each egg, yet still allow salad to be seen.

Press the yolk of the hard-boiled egg through a sieve over the dish, then sprinkle with the parsley and herbs. Garnish dish with watercress, if wanted.

Eggs with tunny fish

3 eggs (hard-boiled)
3-4 tablespoons tunny fish, or
   1 small can (flaked)
$1\frac{1}{2}$ oz creamed butter, or 1
   tablespoon mayonnaise
salt and pepper

For béchamel sauce
$\frac{1}{4}$ pint milk (infused with 1 bay-leaf, 1 blade of mace and 6 peppercorns)
$\frac{1}{2}$ oz butter
1 tablespoon flour

For salad
$\frac{1}{4}$ lb French beans
4 oz black olives (stoned)
$\frac{1}{2}$ lb firm tomatoes (skinned, quartered and seeds removed)
French dressing (lightly flavoured with garlic)

Forcing bag with $\frac{1}{2}$-inch plain nozzle

This makes a good first course for a party meal or summer lunch. Other fish, meat, chicken or ham can be used instead of tunny fish.

Method
For béchamel sauce, make a roux of melted butter and flour, strain on flavoured milk and stir until boiling. Set aside to cool.

Peel and halve the eggs lengthways. Sieve the yolks, then pound them in a basin with the tunny fish, 3 tablespoons of béchamel sauce, and creamed butter or mayonnaise. Season well.

Wash and dry the egg whites, arrange round a serving dish, securing them with a little of the mixture. Put the remaining mixture into the forcing bag and pipe into the whites. Mix the salad ingredients together and pile into the centre of the dish.

Oeufs au cresson

(Egg and watercress mayonnaise)

4-5 eggs (hard-boilled)
1 oz butter
¼ pint thick mayonnaise
salt and pepper
2 bunches of watercress
squeeze of lemon
pinch of cayenne pepper, or 2-3
   drops of Tabasco sauce
1-2 tablespoons French dressing
1 lemon (sliced)

Method

Cut the eggs in half lengthways, remove the yolks and rub them through a wire strainer. Soften the butter, work in the egg yolks and about 1 teaspoon of mayonnaise, season well. Cover the yolk mixture and keep the egg whites in a bowl of cold water.

Boil 1 bunch of watercress for 5 minutes, then drain it well and sieve. Add this watercress purée to the remaining mayonnaise with a squeeze of lemon and cayenne (or Tabasco sauce). Chop the second bunch of watercress coarsely and mix with the French dressing and place in the serving dish.

Dry the egg whites, fill with creamed yolk mixture and reshape eggs. Arrange them on the chopped watercress and coat with the flavoured mayonnaise. Garnish with slices of lemon and serve with brown bread and butter.

Left : making the sauce for oeufs au cresson : the watercress purée is mixed into the mayonnaise before adding a squeeze of lemon juice, and a little cayenne or Tabasco
Right : placing the eggs, filled with creamed yolk and mayonnaise mixture, on a bed of chopped watercress and French dressing

Leek and egg salad

4-5 leeks (according to size)
salt
little French dressing
3 hard-boiled eggs
$\frac{1}{4}$-$\frac{1}{2}$ pint mayonnaise
paprika pepper

Method
Wash the leeks thoroughly. Split in half lengthways and tie together to form a neat bundle. Boil in salted water until just tender (about 12 minutes), drain and refresh. Untie, put in dish and pour over a little French dressing.

Cut white of eggs into strips and scatter over the leeks. Sieve yolks through a wire bowl strainer. Thin the mayonnaise, if necessary, with 1 tablespoon of boiling water. Spoon this over the salad to coat leeks, and sprinkle sieved yolks on top. Dust with paprika pepper and serve lightly chilled.

Egg mousse

12 eggs (hard-boiled)
$\frac{1}{2}$ pint mayonnaise
1 oz gelatine
$\frac{1}{4}$ pint chicken stock, or white wine
cayenne pepper
Worcestershire sauce
anchovy essence
salt
$\frac{1}{4}$ pint double cream (lightly whipped)

For béchamel sauce
1$\frac{1}{2}$ oz butter
1$\frac{1}{2}$ oz flour
$\frac{3}{4}$ pint milk (infused with slice of onion, 6 peppercorns, 1 bayleaf, 1 blade of mace)
salt and pepper

For devil sauce
1 cup of tomatoes (canned), or 3 large ripe tomatoes (skinned and simmered to a pulp)
caster sugar
garlic (to taste)
2 tablespoons oil
1 dessertspoon vinegar
1 tablespoon Worcestershire sauce
1 dessertspoon tomato ketchup
salt and pepper
mustard

6-inch diameter soufflé dish, or cake tin

Method
Chop the eggs and mix with the mayonnaise in a bowl. Prepare the béchamel sauce (see page 137 for method) and cover with well-buttered greaseproof paper to prevent a skin forming, allow to cool.

Dissolve the gelatine in the stock or wine, add to the béchamel sauce and then stir into the mayonnaise and egg mixture. Season well with cayenne, Worcestershire sauce, anchovy essence and salt, and, when mousse is quite cold and thick, fold in whipped cream, using a metal spoon.

Turn into the lightly oiled soufflé dish or cake tin and leave in a cool place to set.

To prepare the devil sauce : mix all ingredients together in the order given. Turn the mousse on to a serving dish ; garnish with one of the alternatives (see right). Serve sauce separately.

Water-thin cucumber slices surround egg mousse, as a finishing touch

Egg mousse garnish

Cucumber Wipe and slice thinly. Make a cut in each slice from the centre to the outside edge. Twist one cut edge away from centre to make slices stand up.
Watercress Wash and trim sprays. Arrange on top of mousse in a small bunch.
Tomato Scald in boiling water. Remove skins and slice across flesh thinly. Arrange round mousse and garnish top with small bunch of watercress and slices of tomato.
Lettuce hearts Wash and chill until crisp, cut in four. Arrange round base and decorate top with cucumber and a spray of watercress.

Melon salad

1 honeydew melon
1 lb tomatoes
1 large cucumber
salt
1 tablespoon chopped parsley
1 heaped teaspoon chopped mint
and chives

For French dressing
2 tablespoons wine vinegar
salt and pepper
caster sugar
6 tablespoons salad oil

Method

Cut the melon in half, remove the seeds and scoop out the flesh with a vegetable cutter or cut into cubes.

Skin and quarter the tomatoes, squeeze out the seeds and remove the core; cut quarters again if the tomatoes are large.

Peel the cucumber, cut in small cubes, or the same size as the melon cubes. Sprinkle lightly with salt, cover with a plate and stand for 30 minutes; drain away any liquid and rinse cubes with cold water.

To prepare the dressing: mix the vinegar, seasoning and sugar together, then whisk in the oil.

Mix the fruit and vegetables together in a deep bowl (or soup tureen), pour over the dressing, cover and chill for 2-3 hours.

Just before serving, mix in the herbs. Serve from the bowl or tureen with a ladle into soup cups.

While standing, the salad will make a lot of juice, so it should be eaten with a spoon. You'll find a hot herb loaf (see right) goes well with melon salad.

Melon salad, an unusual starter

Hot herb loaf

1 French loaf
4 oz butter
1 tablespoon mixed dried herbs
juice of $\frac{1}{4}$ lemon
black pepper
little garlic (crushed) — optional

Method
Set the oven at 425°F or Mark 7. Cream the butter with the herbs, lemon juice and seasoning; if you like garlic, add a little now.

Cut the loaf in even, slanting slices about $\frac{1}{2}$ inch thick; spread each slice generously with the butter mixture and reshape the loaf, spreading any remaining butter over the top and sides before wrapping in foil.

Bake for 10 minutes in the oven at 425°F or Mark 7. Then reduce oven setting to 400°F or Mark 6, and open the foil so that the bread browns and crisps. This should take a further 5-8 minutes.

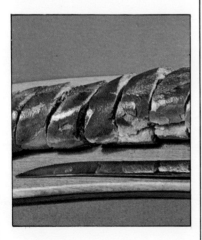

Pineapple japonaise

1 pineapple
little caster sugar
squeeze of lemon juice
tarragon cream dressing
little cream, or top of milk
    (optional)

This is definitely a party dish for serving either as a separate first course or, for example, with cold turkey or chicken.

Method
Split the pineapple in two lengthways and, using a grapefruit knife, slice out the core, then cut out the flesh. Slice this and put it back in the skin. Sprinkle with a little sugar and lemon juice, and chill for 30 minutes. Then coat the pineapple with dressing (if this is too thick, thin with a little extra cream or top of milk) and serve.

Pineapple jelly salad

1 large can (approximately 24 fl oz)
  pineapple juice
juice of 2 large oranges (strained)
2 wineglasses dry white wine, or
  water
1 tablespoon white wine vinegar
1 oz gelatine (soaked in 5-6
  tablespoons cold water)
6 tablespoons canned pineapple
  (diced)
1 bunch of watercress

For dressing
2 packets of Demi-Sel cheese, or
  4 oz cream cheese
$\frac{1}{4}$ pint single cream
salt and pepper

Ring mould (2-2$\frac{1}{2}$ pints capacity)

Method
Combine the pineapple and strained orange juices with the wine (or water) and vinegar in a large pan.

Watchpoint Do not use the syrup from a can of pineapple pieces because this would be too sweet.

Make up this liquid to 1$\frac{1}{2}$ pints with more juice or water, if necessary.

Dissolve the soaked gelatine in a pan and when quite hot add to the liquid ; pour about one-third into the wet mould and leave in a cold place until almost set.

Arrange diced pineapple in the mould and fill up with re-

Arranging diced pineapple over gelatine mixture (which is almost set)

maining cool, but still liquid, jelly. Cover and leave for 2-3 hours in refrigerator or overnight in a cool larder before turning out.

To prepare dressing: rub cheese through a wire strainer into a bowl and beat in the cream a little at a time. Season to taste, then pour the dressing into a small bowl or sauce boat for serving.

Turn out the jelly on to a flat serving plate and fill the centre with watercress.

Watchpoint To turn out the jelly, dip the mould quickly in and out of a bowl containing hot water. Wipe the outside of the mould and then put the plate over the top and turn it upside down. Holding the plate and mould, give them a smart shake from side to side (not up and down, which would spoil the shape), then lift away the mould.

Serve with brown bread and butter and the dressing separately.

Cucumber jelly salad

1 large cucumber
$\frac{3}{4}$ pint clear chicken stock (see page 139)
$\frac{3}{4}$ oz gelatine
scant $\frac{1}{4}$ pint double cream
salt and pepper
paprika pepper
white crab meat (canned, or frozen)
French dressing (spiced with tomato ketchup)
1 lb tomatoes (sliced)

Ring mould (1-1$\frac{1}{4}$ pints capacity)

Method
Cut cucumber into small dice, blanch, refresh and drain thoroughly. Dissolve gelatine in a small quantity of the stock, then add remainder with cream to bowl. Season well. When on the point of setting add the cucumber and turn into a wet mould. Leave to set.

Turn out and fill centre of mould with white crab meat mixed with the spiced French dressing. Surround with the sliced tomatoes and chill the salad before serving.

Grapefruit and green grape salad

3 large grapefruit
6-8 oz green grapes
little caster sugar

For dressing
3-4 tablespoons olive, or salad, oil
about 2 tablespoons lemon juice
caster sugar and salt (to taste)
pepper (ground from mill)
1 teaspoon chopped fresh, or bottled, mint

Choose thin-skinned and heavy grapefruit. This quantity serves 6 people.

Method
Cut each grapefruit in half and prepare in usual way (see page 139). Dip grapes in boiling water, then peel and pip. To remove pips easily, flick them out with pointed end of a potato peeler. Put 1 dessertspoon of grapes in the centre of each grapefruit half. Dust with sugar and chill.

Combine ingredients for dressing, whisk well, taste and correct seasoning. Pour 1 tablespoon of dressing over each grapefruit before serving.

Pears in tarragon cream dressing

3-4 pears
lettuce leaves (optional)
paprika pepper (optional)

For tarragon cream dressing
1 egg
2 rounded tablespoons caster sugar
3 tablespoons tarragon vinegar
salt and pepper
$\frac{1}{4}$ pint double cream

Use ripe, juicy pears such as Comice (one half per person). This quantity serves 6 people.

Method
First prepare dressing : break egg into a bowl and beat with a fork. Add sugar and gradually add the vinegar. Stand bowl in a pan of boiling water. Stir the mixture until beginning to thicken, then draw off heat and continue to stir. When mixture has consistency of thick cream, take basin out of pan, stir for a few seconds longer; season lightly and leave till cold.

Partially whip cream and fold it into the dressing.

Peel pears, cut in half and, with a teaspoon, scoop out cores and fibrous threads which run from core to stalk. If using lettuce leaves, lay one or two on individual serving plates, breaking spines, so that they lie flat. Place a half pear in the centre of each, rounded side up, then coat with 1 tablespoon of dressing. If using paprika, shake a little over the top.

The dressing can be made up (without cream) in large quantities and stored, when cold, in a screw-top jar in the refrigerator. It will keep for up to 3 weeks. Add cream only after taking out of refrigerator.

Pear and walnut salad

1 pear per person

For dressing
1 large egg
2 tablespoons caster sugar
3 tablespoons tarragon vinegar
1 small carton (2½ fl oz) double
  cream

To finish
1 lettuce
3 oz shelled walnuts (roughly
  chopped)

Choose ripe dessert pears such as Comice, William or Packham and allow 1 per person. The quantities are sufficient for 6 pears.

Method
To prepare the dressing: beat the egg and sugar until thoroughly mixed, then add the vinegar. Place the bowl over a saucepan of gently simmering water and stir until the mixture is thick. Remove from the heat and leave until cold. Whip the cream until it just begins to thicken, then fold it into the dressing.

Cut the pears in half, peel them, and scoop out core with a teaspoon. Reshape and place each pear on a crisp lettuce leaf on a salad plate, and immediately spoon over the dressing. Scatter over the roughly chopped walnuts. Serve with brown bread and butter, or cheese sablés (see page 48).

Celery and green pepper chartreuse

1 packet of lime jelly
juice of $\frac{1}{2}$ lemon
1 tablespoon onion juice
1 green pepper
1 cap of canned pimiento
$\frac{1}{4}$ pint mayonnaise
4 sticks of celery (diced)
sprigs of watercress

Ring mould (2$\frac{1}{2}$ pints capacity)

Method

Break the jelly into cubes, pour on $\frac{1}{2}$ pint boiling water, stir until dissolved, then add the lemon and onion juice, and make up to $\frac{3}{4}$ pint with cold water; leave to cool.

Remove the core and seeds from the green pepper and cut the flesh in dice. Blanch these in boiling water for 1 minute, then drain and refresh. Dice the pimiento. When the jelly begins to thicken, whisk vigorously until it looks foamy, then fold in the mayonnaise and the prepared celery, pepper and pimiento. Pour into the mould, cover and leave to set.

When ready to serve, dip the mould quickly in and out of hot water, turn jelly on to a serving platter and garnish with sprigs of watercress.

Folding chopped celery, pepper and pimiento into the whisked jelly and mayonnaise mixture for celery and green pepper chartreuse

Garnishing celery and green pepper chartreuse with sprigs of watercress

Peach salad

1 white-fleshed peach per
   person
lettuce leaves (for serving)

For dressing
1 teaspoon curry powder
2 tablespoons port
1 tablespoon apricot jam
¼ pint double cream

Method
First prepare the dressing:
warm curry powder, port and
jam together until the jam has
melted, then strain mixture
through a piece of muslin.
Whip cream until it begins to
thicken, then stir in the strained
dressing mixture.

Scald and peel the peaches,
cut them in half and remove the
stones. Arrange these peach
halves on the lettuce leaves and
spoon dressing over them.

Tomatoes frankfurter

6 medium, or large, tomatoes
2 frankfurters
6 oz lean sliced ham (shredded)
2 oz Belgian liver sausage
French dressing
chopped herbs
salt and pepper

Method
Scald and skin tomatoes, cut
off tops and scoop out seeds.
Blanch the frankfurters for 5
minutes, cool and slice; mix
with the shredded ham and the
liver sausage cut in large dice.
Moisten with the dressing, add
herbs and season. Fill tomatoes,
replace 'lid' and chill.

Tomatoes with avocado and green pepper

6 even-size ripe tomatoes
1 avocado (peeled and diced)
1 green pepper (chopped and
   blanched)
1-2 spring onions (shredded)
2-3 tablespoons French dressing

Method
Scald and skin tomatoes, cut
off tops and scoop out seeds.

Carefully mix prepared
avocado, pepper and onion
and moisten with French dressing. Fill the tomatoes, replace
tops, arrange on a serving dish
and spoon over a little French
dressing with herbs added.

Salad Clémentine

6 tomatoes
salt and pepper
2 tablespoons salad oil
6 eggs (hard-boiled and sliced)
1 tablespoon capers
1 tablespoon gherkins (sliced)
6 anchovy fillets
brown bread and butter (for
  serving)

For dressing
2 tablespoons wine vinegar
1 teaspoon dry mustard
6 tablespoons salad oil
3 dessertspoons tomato ketchup
1 tablespoon chopped mixed herbs
  (fresh parsley, chives and mint,
  or 1 tablespoon parsley and pinch
  of dried mixed herbs)
salt
black pepper (ground from mill)

Method

Scald and skin the tomatoes, cut in half through the stalk, cut out the small piece of core at the stalk end and remove seeds. Season tomatoes lightly. Heat oil in a pan and sauté tomatoes very quickly on each side; lift them out very carefully and leave to cool.

Arrange the egg slices on a dish, scatter the capers and gherkins over them. Set the tomatoes, cut side down, on top.

Split the anchovies in half and soak them in 2 tablespoons milk to remove excess salt.

Combine the ingredients for the dressing, adding salt and black pepper to taste.

Drain the anchovy fillets and arrange them lattice-wise over the tomatoes; pour over the dressing. Chill salad for 1 hour and serve with brown bread and butter.

Watchpoint Even if very ripe, the tomatoes must be sautéed in oil otherwise they make too much juice after dressing is poured on.

Arranging the anchovy fillets lattice-wise over the tomatoes

The finished dish of salad Clémentine after it has been chilled. It is served with thinly sliced brown bread and butter

Tomatoes Gervais

8 tomatoes
salt and pepper
4 oz cream cheese (2 packets
  Gervais, or loose curd cheese)
small bunch of fresh chives (or
  chopped parsley, or spring
  onion tops, or snipped watercress
  stalks)
2-3 tablespoons double cream, or
  top of milk
watercress (to garnish) — optional
French dressing

A curd cheese such as Gervais is best to use here as it is richer than cottage cheese, but not as rich as the Petit-Suisse type of full cream cheese.

If neither fresh chives nor the A.F.D. (accelerated freeze dried) ones are available and the suggested alternatives are used, then chopped herbs, such as thyme, marjoram or basil, should be added to the dressing.

Method
Scald and skin the tomatoes. Cut a slice from the top (not stalk end) of each tomato, reserve slices; hold tomato in hollow of your palm, flick out seeds with the handle of a teaspoon, using the bowl of the spoon to detach the core. So much the better if the spoon is worn and therefore slightly sharp. Drain the hollowed-out tomatoes and lightly season inside each one with salt.

Sieve the cheese by pushing it through a strainer resting on a bowl, using a wooden spoon or plastic spatula. Season well and add some of the chives (cut finely with scissors), or chopped herbs. Soften with cream or top of the milk.

Fill the tomatoes with this cheese mixture with a teaspoon, replace their top slices on the slant and arrange them in a serving dish.

Make the French dressing and spoon a little over the tomatoes (be sure to reserve some for spooning over at the last moment). Chill up to 2 hours before serving. Garnish with watercress and sprinkle remains of chives over tomatoes. Serve with walnut bread and butter rolls (see page 140).

Tomato with avocado pear salad

5-6 even-size tomatoes (ripe but
  firm)
2 large avocado pears
lemon juice
salt and pepper
dash of Tabasco sauce
4-5 tablespoons French dressing

For serving
brown bread and butter
chopped walnuts

This salad may be served as a
first course or, without the
bread and butter, with cold
roast chicken.

Method
Scald and skin tomatoes, slice
off tops at the smooth end and
carefully scoop out the seeds.
Season inside well with lemon
juice, salt, pepper and Tabasco
and leave to chill for 30 minutes.

Peel the avocado pears and
cut into small dice, using a
stainless steel knife to prevent
discoloration. Season, and mix
the dice with a little French
dressing. Put them into the
tomatoes, replace tops, arrange
on a serving dish and spoon
over the rest of the dressing.

Serve with brown bread and
butter, sprinkled with a few
chopped walnuts and rolled up.

Avocado pear

$\frac{1}{2}$ avocado per person
$\frac{1}{2}$-1 green pepper (enough to
  give 2 tablespoons, chopped)
2 tablespoons chopped spring
  onion
6 black olives (stoned and
  shredded)

For vinaigrette dressing
salt
black pepper (ground from mill)
1$\frac{1}{2}$ tablespoons white wine
  vinegar
5 tablespoons salad oil
squeeze of lemon
caster sugar (to taste)
1 teaspoon chopped parsley

Choose ripe avocado pears,
allowing one half per person.
When ripe the fruit is slightly
soft, and if shaken the stone will
rattle a little. You can buy
avocados a day or two before
needed and leave to ripen in
the dark (in the larder), but take
the advice of your greengrocer
on their state of ripeness.

Method
Drop the chopped green pepper
into boiling water, cook for 1
minute, then drain and rinse well
with cold water.

To make dressing: mix a
large pinch of salt and black
pepper with the vinegar and
whisk in the oil. Sharpen with
lemon juice and add a little
sugar to taste. Add all other
ingredients to this dressing.

Split the avocado pears in
half with a stainless steel or
silver knife and remove the
stone. Fill each half with the
sharp vinaigrette dressing and
chill slightly before serving on
individual plates.

Avocado pears Roquefort

2-3 avocado pears (according to size)
1 small lettuce

For dressing
2 oz Roquefort cheese
1 teaspoon Worcestershire sauce
2 tablespoons double cream
4-5 tablespoons French dressing
$\frac{1}{2}$ teaspoon finely grated onion

Serve as a first course or accompanying salad.

Method
First prepare the dressing. Work the Roquefort until quite smooth, adding the Worcestershire sauce and cream, then gradually the French dressing and finely grated onion.

Prepare the lettuce and arrange in a dish or on individual plates. Peel and quarter the avocado pears, arrange on the lettuce leaves, spoon over the dressing and serve.

Grape aspic salad

$\frac{3}{4}$ lb green grapes (peeled and pipped)
$1\frac{1}{4}$ oz gelatine
$1\frac{1}{4}$ pints water
1 dessertspoon chopped mint
scant $\frac{1}{4}$ pint lemon juice
caster sugar (to taste)
green edible colouring (optional)
watercress
vinaigrette dressing

Ring mould (1$\frac{1}{2}$- 1$\frac{3}{4}$ pints capacity)

Method
Soak the gelatine in a little of the water and dissolve over gentle heat. Add the remaining water, mint and lemon juice. Sweeten to taste and colour liquid a little, if wished.

Pour a little of this liquid into the wet mould; when set, put in the grapes and add enough liquid to cover them. Leave to set. Then fill mould to the brim with the rest of the liquid. Leave to set. Turn out salad, garnish centre with watercress and serve a vinaigrette dressing and brown bread and butter separately.
Note : the jelly should be pleasantly acidulated.

Spiced jellied mushrooms

8 oz mushrooms
1 can turtle soup, or consommé
1 dessertspoon soy sauce
salt and pepper
2-3 drops of Tabasco sauce
dash of Worcestershire sauce
$\frac{1}{2}$ pint water
$\frac{1}{4}$ oz gelatine
lemon juice

To finish
lettuce
lemon quarters
brown bread and butter

Method
Trim mushrooms and wash them, if necessary. Chop the trimmings and put into a pan with the soup or consommé, seasoning, sauces, water and mushrooms. Simmer mixture for 5-10 minutes, then draw it aside. Dissolve gelatine in a little of the liquid from the pan, add this to the mushrooms, adjust seasoning and sharpen with lemon juice. Turn into a flat dish or wet tin and leave to set.

To serve, cut salad across into squares and arrange on lettuce leaves. Serve with lemon quarters and brown bread and butter separately.

Salad japonaise

1 cabbage lettuce
2 oranges
1 small pineapple, or 2-3 slices
of canned pineapple
2-3 tomatoes
tarragon cream dressing
parsley (chopped) — optional

This salad can be made from a variety of fruit in season — ripe pears, stoned cherries and so on.

Serve it also as a side salad with chicken and cold fish dishes.

Method
Wash and dry lettuce, arrange on individual plates, breaking the spine of the leaf so that it will lie flat on the plate. Slice away the peel and white pith from the oranges and, using a sharp knife, peel and slice the fresh pineapple and cut into small pieces (cut canned pineapple in the same way). Scald and quarter the tomatoes and flick out the seeds.

Arrange the oranges, tomatoes and pineapple on the lettuce leaves. Have the cream dressing ready and spoon a little of it on to each salad. Sprinkle each salad with freshly chopped parsley if wished.

Artichokes vinaigrette

4 **globe artichokes**

For vinaigrette dressing
2 **shallots (finely chopped)**
6 **tablespoons olive oil**
2-3 **oz mushrooms (finely chopped)**
3 **tablespoons white wine**
2 **tablespoons white wine vinegar**
salt and pepper
squeeze of lemon juice (optional)
1 **clove of garlic (optional)**
3 **oz ham (thinly sliced and finely chopped)**
1 **tablespoon chopped parsley, or chopped mixed herbs**

Method
Trim off the points and leaves of the artichokes with scissors and trim the stalk from the bottom. Plunge artichokes into boiling salted water and boil gently until a leaf can be pulled out (about 35-40 minutes). Then drain, refresh, and leave until cold.

Meanwhile prepare the dressing. Sauté the shallots slowly until just tender in 2 tablespoons of the oil, add the mushrooms and cook for 2-3 minutes. Turn into a bowl and leave until cool, then add wine, vinegar and remaining oil. Season well and add a squeeze of lemon juice if the dressing is not sharp enough. Flavour with a little garlic, if liked, and add the ham. Leave this to marinate for 15-20 minutes.

Chopped shallots, mushrooms and ham are mixed with wine, vinegar and oil to make a thick dressing for the artichokes

After some of the centre leaves and the chokes have been removed, the vinaigrette dressing is spooned into the centre of the artichokes

Prepare each artichoke by pulling out some of the centre leaves until the choke can be reached ; carefully scrape this away with a dessertspoon. Put a spoonful of the dressing in the centre of each artichoke, set them on individual dishes and dust with the chopped parsley or herbs. Serve cold.

The artichokes, filled with thick dressing, are served on individual plates

Stuffed apple salad

4 even-size dessert apples
2 inner sticks from a head of
celery (shredded)
2 tablespoons cream
1 dessertspoon lemon juice, or
wine vinegar
little caster sugar
black pepper (ground from mill)
salt (optional)
garlic (optional)

To garnish
4 walnut halves

Method

Shred celery sticks very finely
and place in a bowl of ice-cold
water so that they curl.

Choose apples of a pippin
variety with unblemished skins.
Wipe and polish them with a
soft cloth. Cut off tops and carefully scoop out the flesh without
breaking the skin. Remove cores
and seeds, chop the flesh and
place in a bowl.

Drain and dry shredded celery.
Add to the chopped apple and
mix well.

Blend cream, lemon juice or
wine vinegar and seasonings
together and pour over the apple
and celery. Stir carefully until
fruit is well coated with dressing.
Watchpoint If the dressing is
stirred vigorously, it will become
too thick and may curdle.

Spoon mixture into apple
cases and decorate each apple
with a walnut half. Serve with
cheese sablés.

Cheese sablés

3 oz cheese (grated)
3 oz plain flour (sifted)
3 oz butter
salt and pepper
1 egg (lightly beaten)

Method

Sift flour into a bowl. Cut butter
into flour with a palette knife
and, as soon as pieces are well
coated with flour, rub in with
your fingertips until mixture
resembles fine breadcrumbs.

Add cheese and season to
taste. Press mixture together to
make a dough. Flour, wrap dough
in greaseproof paper, chill in
refrigerator. Set oven at 375°F
or Mark 5.

Carefully roll out pastry mixture
into a fairly thin oblong, flouring
rolling pin well because this
pastry tends to stick ; if it does,
ease it free with a palette knife.
Cut into strips about 2 inches
wide. Brush with beaten egg and
cut strips into triangles.

Place sablés on a baking
sheet lined with greaseproof
paper, and cook in the pre-set
oven for 10 minutes until golden-
brown.

Watchpoint Take baking sheet
out of oven at once. Lift off
greaseproof paper, with cooked
sablés on it. Cheese scorches
easily so that if you remove
them from tray one by one, the
last biscuits could become
scorched through over-cooking.

Serve the sablés cold.

Roquefort salad

1¼ lb small new potatoes
4-6 oz thin streaky bacon rashers
  (green)

For dressing
2 oz Roquefort cheese
7 tablespoons French dressing
salt and pepper
¼ pint double cream
watercress (to garnish)

Method
Boil the potatoes in their skins. Meanwhile, shred the bacon and fry until crisp. Peel the potatoes while still hot, slice and moisten with some of the French dressing. Add the crispy pieces of bacon and season.

Crush the Roquefort well and work in remainder of French dressing and the cream. Dish up potatoes and coat with dressing. Garnish with watercress.

Tomatoes with Roquefort cream

8 even-size tomatoes
salt and pepper
2 eggs (hard-boiled)
3 sticks of tender celery (taken from centre of the head) — finely diced
3 oz Roquefort cheese
2 tablespoons double cream
4 tablespoons French dressing
1 teaspoon chopped chives

Method
Scald and skin tomatoes. Cut off the tops from the smooth end and carefully scoop out the seeds and core, using a teaspoon, drain and season the insides.

Chop the whites of the hard-boiled eggs and mix with the celery. Sieve the cheese and work half with the cream in a bowl. Combine celery mixture with this cheese and fill into the tomatoes; replace the tops of the tomatoes 'on the slant'. Work the French dressing into the remaining cheese and add the chives.

Sieve the egg yolks on to a serving dish, set tomatoes on top and spoon over the dressing.

Cassolettes of cucumber

3-4 cucumbers (according to size)
croûtes of toast, or fried bread
pimiento, or strips of chilli skin
   (to decorate)
1 pint aspic jelly (see page 136)
small cress (to garnish)

Fluted and plain cutters

Method

Cut the cucumbers in 1-inch thick slices, stamp into cases using a fluted cutter for the outside and a smaller, plain one for the inside; do not cut all the way through as cases must have bases. Discard seeds. Cook cucumber cases in boiling salted water for 5 minutes, then drain and refresh them. Prepare the fillings (see right).

Then place each cucumber case on a croûte and fill with the chosen mixture, doming it slightly on top. Decorate with rounds of pimiento or crossed strips of chilli skin and baste with cold liquid aspic. Garnish cases with cress and serve them well chilled.

> **Cassolettes** are individual containers (casseroles) and this recipe is so called because the cucumber cases take the place of true cassolettes.

Mushroom filling

4 oz mushrooms
1 oz butter
1 teaspoon flour
3-4 tablespoons milk, or stock
salt and pepper
1 teaspoon chopped mint

Method

Wash mushrooms and chop finely. Melt butter, add mushrooms and cook until all the moisture has been driven off. Draw pan aside, stir in the flour and milk (or stock). Season and bring mixture to the boil. Add the chopped mint and allow mixture to cool before putting it into the cucumber cases.

Cheese and shrimp filling

1 packet of Demi-Sel, or cream, cheese (2-3 oz)
salt and pepper
4 oz shelled shrimps

Method

Work the cream cheese with seasoning to taste and add the shelled shrimps.

Chicken and ham or tongue filling

2 oz cooked chicken (minced)
2 oz cooked ham, or tongue (minced)
1 anchovy fillet (minced)
mayonnaise (to bind)
salt and pepper

Method

Mix the chicken, ham (or tongue) and anchovy, bind with mayonnaise and season well.

Salad Alice

3 Cox's apples
1 head of celery
$\frac{1}{2}$ lb chicory
1 oz almonds (blanched, split
   and soaked)

For dressing
2 oz Gorgonzola cheese
$\frac{1}{4}$ pint double cream
salt and pepper
caster sugar (to taste)
lemon juice (to taste)

Method

Quarter and core the apples. Cut the celery into small sticks and the chicory leaves into 2-inch lengths. Put into a bowl, slice in the apples and add the almonds.

To make the dressing: work the Gorgonzola until soft and add the cream gradually. Season well, adding sugar and lemon juice to taste. Mix dressing into the salad ingredients and pile into a salad bowl for serving.

Endives ardennaise

5 good heads of chicory
2-3 tablespoons water
squeeze of lemon juice
little grated cheese and melted
   butter (for browning)

For sauce
good $\frac{1}{2}$ oz butter
scant $\frac{1}{2}$ oz flour
$\frac{1}{2}$ pint milk
1$\frac{1}{2}$ oz grated cheese (Gruyère and
   Parmesan mixed, or dry
   Cheddar)
$\frac{1}{2}$ teaspoon French, or made
   English, mustard
salt and pepper
2 oz lean cooked ham (cut in
   julienne strips)

'Endive' is known in Britain as chicory, and is conical shaped with tightly packed white leaves. Confusion often arises because the salad vegetable known in Britain as endive is called 'chicorée' in France. British chicory should be used in this recipe.

Method

Set oven at 400°F or Mark 6. Trim the chicory, put into a well-buttered flameproof casserole with the water and lemon juice. Cover with a piece of buttered paper and the lid. Set on a low heat for 5-6 minutes, then put into the oven for 45-50 minutes until the chicory is clear-looking and very tender.

Meanwhile prepare a sauce with the butter, flour and milk and beat in the cheese with the seasonings. Stir the ham into this sauce. Lift the chicory on to a serving dish, coat with the sauce, dust well with the grated cheese, sprinkle with melted butter and brown under the grill.

Main course salads

When the weather is mild, be it summer or any other time of the year, a salad is welcome as a lunch or supper dish. If vegetables and fruit are combined with meat, cheese, fish or eggs you have a dish that is a well balanced meal in itself, full of vitamins and minerals as well as protein. If the chosen salad seems a little on the light side, serve a soup beforehand.

These salads are often an attractive and appetising way of using up the rest of the joint or making use of some of the cans from the store cupboard. If using leftover meat, slice or dice it neatly and marinate it in a little French dressing, even if the salad is to be dressed with mayonnaise. This gives extra moistness and flavour to the meat.

On a grander scale, meat and fish salads form the basis of many a buffet meal for parties. The jellies and mousses on pages 56 to 66 are particularly suitable for this as they are decorative, unusual and easy to eat when seating accomodation may not be over-generous. If you can offer more than one on your cold table, so much the better.

The same rules apply to savoury jellies as to sweet ones — use as little gelatine as possible to obtain a light set, and do not prepare them too far in advance. A jelly that stands for more than 24 hours will gradually set firmer and firmer and become more and more unpalatable.

Finally, don't forget that with a light salad as your main course, you must choose a light wine, or the flavour will be drowned.

Cucumber and cheese mousse

1 large cucumber
6 oz curd, or cream, cheese
1 teaspoon onion juice (from
    finely grated onion)
salt and white pepper
$\frac{1}{4}$ pint boiling water, or vegetable
    or chicken stock
$\frac{1}{2}$ oz gelatine (soaked in 3
    tablespoons cold water)
2 tablespoons white wine
    vinegar
1 tablespoon caster sugar
pinch of ground mace, or
    coriander
$\frac{1}{4}$ pint double cream (lightly
    whipped)

For garnish
1 bunch of watercress

For serving
1 large green pepper
$\frac{1}{4}$ pint French dressing
brown bread and butter

Ring mould (1$\frac{1}{2}$-2 pints capacity)

Method
First oil the ring mould. Dice the cucumber very finely, sprinkle with salt and leave it pressed between two plates for 30 minutes. Work the cheese with onion juice and seasoning. Pour boiling water (or stock) on to soaked gelatine, stir until it is dissolved, then add it to cheese.

Drain the diced cucumber thoroughly and mix it with vinegar, sugar and spice. When the cheese mixture is quite cold, fold in the cucumber and the cream. Pour into the prepared mould and leave to set.

Wash and pick over the watercress. Chop the green pepper, blanch in boiling water and refresh it.

Turn out the mousse. Fill the centre with watercress. Add the prepared green pepper to the French dressing and serve this separately with brown bread and butter.

Lobster mousse

1 large live lobster (weight
  about 2 lb)
2 pints court bouillon (for
  cooking lobster — see page 138)
$\frac{1}{2}$ pint velouté sauce (made with
  1 oz butter, 1 oz flour, $\frac{1}{2}$ pint
  court bouillon in which lobster
  has been cooked) — see page 140
$\frac{1}{2}$ oz gelatine
3 eggs (hard-boiled)
$7\frac{1}{2}$ fl oz mayonnaise
$2\frac{1}{2}$ fl oz court bouillon
$2\frac{1}{2}$ fl oz double cream
  (lightly whipped)

salt
paprika pepper

To finish
$2\frac{1}{2}$ fl oz thick mayonnaise
2-3 tablespoons tomato juice
sprigs of watercress (picked
  over)
head shell of lobster (split in two
  and lightly oiled)

*7-inch diameter top (No. 1 size)
  soufflé dish, or cake tin*

Crab mousse

Method

Lightly oil the dish or tin. Cook the lobster in the court bouillon for 30 minutes and leave to cool in the liquid.

Prepare the velouté sauce and leave to cool, covered with a buttered greaseproof paper to prevent a skin forming.

Shell the lobster, cut the tail meat in slices, chop the claw meat and scoop out all the soft creamy meat from the head, first removing the sac containing weed. Oil and split the head shell of the lobster, and set aside. Shell the eggs, chop the whites and sieve the yolks. Soak the gelatine in the $2\frac{1}{2}$ fl oz court bouillon, then dissolve it over gentle heat.

Mix the velouté sauce, mayonnaise, egg yolks and whites, gelatine and the claw and soft creamy meat together, and season to taste. When the mixture begins to thicken, fold in the cream and pour mousse into the oiled dish or tin, leave it in a cool place to set.

For serving : turn out the mousse, coat with the mayonnaise, thinned with the tomato juice, and arrange the slices of lobster on top. Garnish with the head shell and watercress.

1 lb crab meat ($\frac{1}{2}$ white, $\frac{1}{2}$ dark)
$\frac{1}{2}$ pint velouté sauce (made with 1 oz butter, 1 oz flour, $\frac{1}{2}$ pint court bouillon, or light chicken stock) — see page 140
$\frac{1}{2}$ oz gelatine
$2\frac{1}{2}$ fl oz white wine
$\frac{1}{2}$ pint mayonnaise
$\frac{1}{4}$ pint double cream (lightly whipped)

For garnish
1 cucumber
4 tablespoons French dressing
$\frac{1}{2}$ teaspoon paprika pepper
Tabasco sauce

7-inch diameter top (No. 1 size) soufflé dish, or cake tin

Method

Oil the dish or tin. Prepare the velouté sauce, work in the dark crab meat and leave to cool. Soak the gelatine in wine, dissolve it over heat and then stir it into velouté sauce with the mayonnaise. Fold the flaked white crab meat into the mixture with the cream. Turn mousse into the prepared dish or tin and leave it to set.

Meanwhile, slice the cucumber, and dégorge. Flavour the French dressing with paprika and a good dash of Tabasco and mix with cucumber. Turn mousse on to a serving dish and spoon cucumber over it.

◀ *Some of the raw ingredients for making a lobster mousse*

Salmon salad en gelée

1 lb salmon steak
1½ pints water
juice of ¼ lemon
1 teaspoon salt
6 white peppercorns
bouquet garni

For wine jelly
2 pints jellied chicken stock (this
    must be the cooking liquor from
    a boiled chicken, flavoured with
    onion, carrot and celery)
salt and pepper
scant ½ oz gelatine
7½ fl oz dry white wine
1 dessertspoon tarragon vinegar
2 egg whites
3 tablespoons chopped parsley

For serving
¼ pint mayonnaise
2 tablespoons double cream
    (whipped)

Method

Wash the fish and dry well. Bring the water and flavourings to the boil, draw aside and leave for 5 minutes. Put the salmon into the hot liquid, cover and bring slowly to the boil again. Reduce the heat, cover the pan and simmer for 15 minutes.

Watchpoint The water must just tremble during this cooking time, not boil, or it will toughen the flesh of the salmon.

Allow the fish to cool a little before draining off the liquid and removing the skin and bones.

To make wine jelly : make sure that the chicken stock is free of fat, season it very well, put it into a large scalded pan and add the gelatine (previously soaked in the wine) and vinegar. To clarify the stock : whisk egg whites to a froth, add them to the stock in the pan and whisk with a backward movement until stock is hot. Bring to the boil, allowing liquid to rise to top of pan, then remove from heat and allow liquid to settle for 5 minutes. Then bring back to the boil, strain through a scalded cloth and leave to cool.

Flake the salmon carefully and turn it into a glass bowl, cover with the cold but still liquid wine jelly and leave to set. Add the parsley to the remaining jelly and, when on the point of setting, pour carefully into the bowl. Leave the salad for 2 hours in a cool place before serving.

Serve with the mayonnaise lightened with the cream.

Jellied tongue salad

½ lb cooked ox tongue
1 can consommé
1 wineglass dry sherry
1 rounded teaspoon gelatine
2 tablespoons water
½ lb small new potatoes
2 tablespoons white wine
salt and pepper
1 small bunch of radishes
2 tablespoons double cream

For dressing
grated rind and juice of ½ orange
salt and pepper
1 teaspoon wine vinegar
4-5 tablespoons olive oil

To garnish
1 bunch of watercress

Ring mould (1½ pints capacity)

Method

Cut tongue into thick julienne strips. Heat the consommé and add the sherry. Soak the gelatine in the water for 5 minutes, then add to hot consommé and stir until it is dissolved; leave to cool.

Put the shredded tongue in the mould and when the consommé is quite cold, but still liquid, spoon it in to fill the mould; put in a cool place for 2 hours to set.

Wash and pick over the watercress. Scrape and cook the new potatoes and while still hot sprinkle with the white wine, salt and pepper. Wash and trim the radishes and leave in ice-cold water for 10-15 minutes, then drain and slice. Mix the potatoes and radishes together, add the cream and turn into a serving dish.

Mix the grated orange rind with seasoning, vinegar and strained orange juice. Whisk in the olive oil until the dressing thickens, taste for seasoning and pour into a sauce boat.

Turn the tongue jelly on to a serving plate and fill the centre with watercress; serve with orange dressing.

Tongue mousse

½ lb ox tongue (cooked)
2 oz ham (cooked)
½ pint béchamel sauce (made
   with ¾ oz butter, ¾ oz flour,
   ½ pint flavoured milk)
¼ pint mayonnaise
½ oz gelatine (dissolved in 5
   tablespoons stock)
3 tablespoons double cream
   (lightly whipped)
1 egg white (stiffly whisked)

For garnish
4 tomatoes
4 oz French beans
½ cucumber
8 black olives
4 tablespoons French dressing

6-inch diameter top (No. 2 size)
soufflé dish

Method

Oil the soufflé dish. Mince the tongue and ham. Prepare béchamel sauce (see method, page 137) and leave to cool. When sauce is cold, beat it into the meat, add mayonnaise and dissolved gelatine. Fold cream into mixture, then fold in whisked egg white (the latter improves texture of tongue mousse because the meat is close-textured).

Turn mousse into oiled dish and leave it to set.

Meanwhile, prepare garnish : scald, skin and quarter tomatoes. Cut the beans into large diamonds and boil until tender ; drain and refresh. Peel and shred cucumber and stone the olives. Mix them all together and moisten with French dressing. Turn out mousse and garnish.

Veal parisienne

1 lb veal pie meat (diced)
1 egg (hard-boiled)
1 teaspoon finely chopped
   parsley
4 oz green streaky bacon
   (blanched and finely shredded)
salt and pepper
¾ pint chicken stock (see page 139)
¼ oz gelatine

For garnish
lettuce hearts (small)
watercress

6-inch diameter cake tin

Method

Set oven at 325°F or Mark 3. Peel and slice the egg. Decorate the bottom of the tin with egg and parsley.

Mix veal and bacon together, season and add any remaining pieces of egg. Mix meats thoroughly with ½ pint of chicken stock and spoon this mixture carefully into the tin.

Cover tin with a double thickness of greaseproof paper or foil and bake in the pre-set oven for 1½-2 hours.

Dissolve the gelatine in the remaining stock, season well and strain this liquid into the tin.

When cold and set, turn veal on to a serving dish and garnish with lettuce and watercress. Serve with potato mayonnaise (page 102) or tomato salad with lemon dressing (page 113).

Spooning the veal and bacon, mixed with chicken stock, on top of the egg and parsley which have been arranged in the tin. Extra stock will be used for the jelly

Below : veal parisienne garnished with lettuce and watercress

Chartreuse of spring vegetables

1 bunch of small new carrots
1 bundle of asparagus, or sprue
1 lb ripe tomatoes
$\frac{1}{2}$ lb French beans
$\frac{3}{4}$ lb small (young) broad beans
$\frac{1}{2}$ lb cooked chicken meat
(shredded)
1$\frac{1}{2}$ pints chicken aspic (cool) — see
page 136

*7-8 inch diameter cake tin, or deep
8-inch diameter sandwich tin*

This is a good and decorative
dish for a fork lunch or supper,
and may be made either of all
vegetables, or vegetables and
shredded, cooked chicken if you
want a more substantial dish.

For a delicate flavour use
chicken aspic but, if time presses,
canned consommé can be used
as a substitute, though the
result will not be as good.

Method

Trim and peel carrots, leave on
about $\frac{1}{4}$ inch of the top. Boil
them until barely tender, then
drain, refresh and drain them
again.

Prepare asparagus or sprue
(see page 136) and tie in bundles.
Cook as for the carrots. Scald,
skin and quarter tomatoes, cut
away the little piece of stalk and
flick out the seeds.

Top, tail and string the French
beans, cut them in half and boil
gently until just tender, drain
and refresh them. Pod and boil
broad beans.

Make sure the tin is scru-
pulously clean. Run a good
$\frac{1}{4}$-$\frac{1}{2}$ inch of the cool aspic into
the bottom of the tin and leave
it to set. Then arrange the
different vegetables on the jelly
to make a pleasing pattern, as
shown in the photograph.

Alternatively, start with an
outer ring of the quartered
tomatoes, an inner ring of asparagus, then carrots, French beans
and, finally, the broad beans.
Spoon over just enough cool

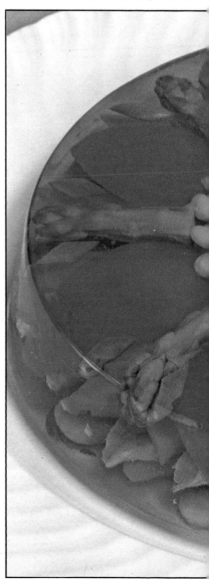

aspic to set the vegetables in position. When set, put in the chicken and any remaining aspic so that it barely covers the top. Leave to set. Then turn out the chartreuse and serve with a potato mayonnaise.

Note : you can use any vegetables in season so long as they make a good contrast in colour and flavour.

Tomato chartreuse

1 large can tomatoes (1¾ pints)
strip of lemon rind
1 teaspoon tomato purée
1 clove of garlic (bruised)
1 bayleaf
salt and granulated sugar (to taste)
6 peppercorns
¼ pint white wine, or water
1½ oz gelatine

Suggested garnish

young carrots and turnips, spring
    onions ; radishes ; celery — for
    dressings, see recipe
French dressing
mint (chopped)
French mustard
grated rind of ½ orange
cream cheese
a little top of milk
parsley (chopped)

Ring mould (about 2 pints capacity)

Trimming carrots into barrel shapes for tomato chartreuse

Method

Put tomatoes in their juice in a pan with lemon rind, purée, seasonings and sugar and bring slowly to boil. Simmer for 3-4 minutes, then press tomato pulp through a nylon strainer.

Add the wine (or water) to gelatine, allow to soak for 3-4 minutes then turn into the hot tomato mixture and stir until gelatine is dissolved. Measure liquid and make up to 2 pints with cold water. Taste for seasoning and pour into a wet ring mould and leave to set.

Prepare and cook vegetables — leave carrots and turnips whole or trim into barrel shapes, depending on their size. Dress as follows :

Carrots : add a lot of chopped mint to a little French dressing and marinate the carrots in this.

Adding the wine and gelatine to the hot tomato mixture

Turnips : to a little French dressing, add 1 dessertspoon French mustard and grated rind of ½ orange. Put in the turnips.
Celery : thin the cream cheese with a little top of the milk, season and add shredded celery and chopped parsley.
Spring onions : trim, blanch in boiling water and serve cold, or keep them raw.

Radishes : cut into 'roses' and soak for about 1 hour in ice-cold water.

Then turn out the tomato jelly when set and surround with the different vegetables. The centre of the mould may be filled with watercress or with shredded chicken bound with mayonnaise, ham cornets stuffed with cream cheese and walnuts, or prawns and shredded pimiento.

Serve a hot savoury roll separately, with a sauce boat of French dressing or mayonnaise.

Note : broad beans, peas, and small new potatoes may also be used to surround the chartreuse.

Tomato chartreuse with prawns

For chartreuse

$\frac{3}{4}$ pint tomato juice, or 1 pint canned tomatoes
strip of lemon rind
$\frac{1}{2}$-1 teaspoon tomato purée
3-4 peppercorns
1 bayleaf
1 clove of garlic (well bruised)
salt
granulated sugar (to taste)
pepper (freshly ground from mill)
$\frac{1}{2}$ oz gelatine (softened in 2-3 tablespoons cold water)
lemon juice (to taste)

For dressing

2 tablespoons wine vinegar
6 tablespoons olive oil
salt, pepper and mustard (to taste)
1$\frac{1}{2}$ oz walnuts (ground through nut mill)
6 oz prawns, or shrimps (shelled)

To garnish
watercress

Ring mould (2$\frac{1}{2}$ pints capacity)

Method

First prepare the chartreuse. Put the tomato juice or canned tomatoes into a pan with the lemon rind, tomato purée, peppercorns, bayleaf, garlic, salt, sugar and pepper to taste. Bring slowly to the boil. Simmer gently for 5 minutes. Strain the juice or press the pulp through a strainer into a measure. If it does not make $\frac{3}{4}$ pint, make it up to this amount with water. Now stir in the softened gelatine, adjust the seasoning and add lemon juice. Cool, pour into a wet ring mould and leave to set.

Combine the vinegar, oil and seasonings for the dressing. Then add the ground walnuts and the shelled prawns or shrimps. Turn out the chartreuse, arrange the watercress in the centre and serve the dressing separately.

Fruit salad platter

1 Webb's lettuce
½ fresh, or 4 rings of canned, pineapple
2 oranges
1 grapefruit
2 tomatoes
2 teaspoons snipped chives
2 tablespoons double cream
1 packet (3-4 oz) of cream, cottage, or lactic, cheese
salt
2 dessert pears
2 peaches
juice of ½ lemon
2 teaspoons chopped mint

Method

Wash and dry the lettuce well, wrap in a cloth or absorbent paper and leave in the refrigerator to crisp while preparing the fruit.

If using fresh pineapple, cut away the skin (see page 91), slice flesh in rings and stamp out the core with a small cutter. Peel the oranges and grapefruit, divide into segments and remove all the membranes. Scald the tomatoes, skin and cut in slices. Work the chives and cream with the cheese and add salt to taste.

Divide the lettuce between four plates, place a ring of pineapple in the middle of each bed of lettuce and put a good tablespoon of the cheese on top. Arrange the prepared oranges, grapefruit and tomatoes around these rings.

Peel the pears and peaches, cut in halves and remove cores and stones. Mix the lemon juice and mint together, spoon this mixture over the pears and peaches, then carefully place half a pear and half a peach on each plate.

Vinaigrette salad

3 medium-size beetroots (cooked)
4-5 medium-size potatoes
1 small head, or 2-3 sticks, of celery
1 large apple
1 pickled dill cucumber
salt and pepper
1 cup of peas (cooked)
1 large cup of cooked meat, or fish (shredded, or flaked)
¼ pint French dressing
½-¾ pint mayonnaise

This is one of the best salads and ideal for using up leftovers. In addition to the basic mixture of vegetables you can use meat, chicken, fish or shellfish.

Method

Peel the beetroots and cut into dice. Cook potatoes in their skins, peel and cut into dice while still warm. Dice celery. Peel core and dice apple, and dice dill cucumber. Mix all these ingredients together and season very well.

Fork in the peas and meat or fish. Moisten well with French dressing. Cover bowl and leave for 2-3 hours or overnight. To serve, pile up in a dish or salad bowl and coat well with the mayonnaise.

Decorate, if you wish, with sliced dill cucumber, curled celery, prawns, slices of salami or garlic sausage.

Watchpoint Unless using shellfish this salad is best made the day before so that flavours can blend well together. It will keep for 2-3 days in a covered bowl in a refrigerator.

Lobster salad Valencia

2 live lobsters ($\frac{3}{4}$ lb each)
2 pints court bouillon (see page 138)
pinch of saffron
1 cucumber
1 red and 1 green pepper
  (blanched)
1 lb tomatoes (skinned, seeds
  removed)
$\frac{1}{2}$ lb long grain rice

Method
Cook the lobsters in court bouillon for 15 minutes and allow to cool in the liquid.

Soak the saffron in a very little water; slice the cucumber and sprinkle with salt, cover and leave for about 30 minutes in a cool place. Shred the peppers and roughly chop the tomatoes.

Cook the rice in boiling water and the saffron liquid, drain, rinse and dry thoroughly.

Cut the lobster meat in neat, even-size pieces and mix with the rice and vegetables. Serve with romesco sauce.

Romesco sauce

4 tomatoes
2 cloves of garlic (peeled)
2 large red peppers
8-10 toasted almonds
salt and pepper
$\frac{1}{2}$ pint olive oil
wine vinegar (to taste)

Method
Bake tomatoes, garlic and peppers in a moderate oven at 375°F or Mark 5 for 20-25 minutes or until soft. Skin and seed tomatoes and peppers and pound to a smooth paste in a mortar with garlic and almonds. Season, then add the oil, drop by drop, followed by the vinegar.

Allow to stand a little then strain and beat before serving.

Vinaigrette de sole aux ananas

2 soles (each weighing $1\frac{1}{4}$ lb
  filleted)
$2\frac{1}{2}$ fl oz water
juice of $\frac{1}{2}$ lemon
slice of onion
salt
6 peppercorns
1 lb small new potatoes
5 tablespoons French dressing
1 fresh pineapple (peeled and cut
  in slices — see page 91), or 4
  slices of canned pineapple
little caster sugar
paprika pepper
$\frac{1}{2}$ lb tomatoes (skinned)
1 tablespoon chopped parsley

Method
Set oven at 350°F or Mark 4. Roll the fillets of sole and poach them in the water, with a little lemon juice, onion slice and seasoning, in pre-set oven for 10-12 minutes. When cooked, take out and leave to cool in the liquid.

Meanwhile cook the potatoes in their skins; then peel, slice and sprinkle with French dressing while still hot. Season pineapple with a little lemon juice, sugar and paprika. Cut the tomatoes in four, remove the seeds and then cut flesh into strips. Arrange the potato salad down the centre of a serving dish, drain the sole and arrange on top. Surround with the pineapple slices. Mix the tomatoes with remaining French dressing and parsley and spoon them over the fish.

Peeling cooked new potatoes to form base for vinaigrette de sole

Placing fillets on potatoes before arranging tomatoes on top

Vinaigrette de sole aux ananas, showing ingredients arranged for serving

Prawn salad

½ lb prawns (shelled)
1 Cantaloupe, or Honeydew, melon
1 lb tomatoes
little caster sugar
6 tablespoons French dressing
1 Webb's, or Cos, lettuce
1 tablespoon mixed chopped herbs (parsley, thyme, chives and mint)

For sauce
½ pint mayonnaise
1 teaspoon dry mustard

Method
Cut melon in half and discard the seeds ; cut the flesh in cubes, mix with the prawns and set aside. Scald and skin the tomatoes, cut in thin slices and arrange, overlapping, around a serving dish or salad bowl. Dust tomatoes lightly with caster sugar and spoon over a little of the French dressing. Shred the lettuce very finely and place in the middle of the dish.

Add mixed herbs to the remaining French dressing and pour it over the prawns and melon ; pile mixture on top of the lettuce.

Mix the mustard to a paste with a little water, add the mayonnaise and then about 1 tablespoon · of boiling water. Serve in a sauce boat.

Sardine salad

1 large can sardines
1 small onion
1 lb tomatoes
2 tablespoons capers
4 tablespoons French dressing
1 tablespoon chopped parsley

Method
Drain the sardines, split, and remove the centre bones. Grate onion ; scald, skin and slice the tomatoes.

Put a layer of sliced tomatoes in an entrée dish, sprinkle half the grated onion and half the capers over them and cover with a layer of sardines. Arrange the remaining tomatoes in a layer on top, cover with the rest of the onion, capers and sardines. Spoon the French dressing over all and dust top with chopped parsley.

Tunny fish salad

1 can (7½ oz) tunny fish
1 dessert apple
2 cooked potatoes (diced)
2 sticks of celery (diced)
1 small can (7½ oz) beetroot, or
  ½ jar small whole beetroot (diced)
1 small can (5 oz) peas, or small
  packet of frozen peas

For dressing
3 tablespoons salad cream
2 tablespoons double cream, or
  evaporated milk, or plain yoghourt
salt and pepper
caster sugar (to taste)
¼ clove of garlic (crushed) —
  optional

For garnish
½ lettuce, or 1 bunch of
  watercress
2 tomatoes (sliced)

Method
Drain the tunny fish, put it into a bowl and flake with a fork.

Peel, core and dice apple. Add apple and potato to tunny fish.

To prepare the dressing : mix salad cream and cream (or evaporated milk or yoghourt) together, season with a little extra salt and pepper and sugar, and the garlic, if liked.

Pour the dressing over the mixture in the bowl and mix carefully with a fork. Turn salad into a serving dish and add the celery, beetroot and peas. Surround with lettuce hearts (or watercress) and tomato slices.

Tunny fish salad makes a filling cold supper (or lunch) dish

Hollandaise salad

3-4 fillets of smoked herring
(according to size), or herring
preserved in white wine
$\frac{1}{2}$ lb long grain Patna rice
1 tablespoon oil
2 dessert apples

For dressing
1 tablespoon mixed mustard
1 tablespoon vinegar
3-4 tablespoons olive oil
salt
pepper (ground from mill)

Method
If using smoked herring, soak
in milk for about 1 hour to
plump up the fillets. Dry these
on absorbent paper and trim
them into diagonal strips.

To prepare the dressing:
combine the ingredients and
season well. Put the pieces of
herring in a dish and spoon
over half the dressing.

Then boil the rice in plenty of
salted water with the oil. After
about 12 minutes, when it is
just tender, drain, rinse with a
little hot water and drain again.
Spread the rice on a baking
sheet and leave in an airy place
to dry. When quite dry but still
tepid, turn into a bowl and
moisten with some dressing.

Pile up the pieces of herring
(without their dressing) in the
bowl with the rice. Quarter and
core the apples (do not peel).
Slice and arrange them over the
rice. Spoon all remaining dressing over the apples. Chill this
salad before serving.

Devilled tunny fish salad

1 can ($7\frac{1}{2}$ oz) tunny fish
1 tablespoon red wine vinegar
1 teaspoon French mustard
2 tablespoons tomato ketchup
3 tablespoons olive oil
salt and pepper
12 oz French beans (fresh, or
frozen)
$\frac{1}{2}$ cucumber
$\frac{1}{2}$ teaspoon caster sugar

To garnish
1 hard-boiled egg and 1 teaspoon
chopped parsley, or 6 anchovy
fillets (split) and 6 black olives
(stoned)

Method
Drain the tunny fish and flake
carefully with two forks. Mix
the vinegar, mustard and ketchup together and whisk in the
oil. Season to taste. Spoon this
mixture over the tunny fish and
leave to marinate while preparing the vegetables and the
garnish.

Trim the French beans and
cut into large diamond-shaped
pieces, cook until just tender
in boiling, salted water, then
drain and refresh. Peel and slice
the cucumber, sprinkle lightly
with salt and leave pressed
between two plates for 15
minutes. Drain cucumber, dust
with caster sugar and pepper.

Put a layer of French beans
at the bottom of an entrée dish,
cover with a layer of the devilled
tunny fish and repeat this until
the dish is full, ending with the
fish. Cover the dish with the
sliced cucumber.

To garnish the dish, either
decorate the top with bands
of egg white (chopped and
mixed with parsley) and egg
yolk (rubbed through a wire

strainer), or make a lattice pattern of anchovy fillets and black olives.

Devilled tunny fish salad, decorated with chopped egg white mixed with parsley, and egg yolk

Crab and rice salad

4-5 oz canned crab claw meat
6 oz long grain Patna rice
1 green, or red, pepper
   (shredded)
salt and pepper
1 clove of garlic (cut)
3 oz black olives (stoned)
2 oz button mushrooms (thinly
   sliced)
1 oz walnut kernels (coarsely
   chopped)

For dressing
juice of 1 small lemon
3-4 tablespoons olive oil
salt
pepper (ground from mill)

Method

Turn out the crab meat and flake with a fork. Boil the rice until tender (about 12 minutes), drain, rinse with a little hot water and drain again. Spread rice on a baking sheet and leave in an airy place to dry. Shred and blanch the pepper.

Combine the ingredients for the dressing. Rub the cut clove of garlic round the serving dish.

While the rice is still warm, season it well with the salt and pepper and mix with the dressing. When quite cold, stir in the crab meat, shredded pepper, olives and raw mushrooms. Fork up well to mix thoroughly, scattering walnuts over the top to serve.

Shredding red pepper for crab and rice salad, with raw sliced mushrooms and stoned olives ready for mixing into salad

Mixing olives with cold rice, crab meat and red pepper before decorating with walnuts

Stuffed eggs aurore

6 eggs (hard-boiled)
3 oz butter
2 caps of pimiento (canned)
salt and pepper
mayonnaise (made with 2 egg yolks, salt, pepper, dry mustard, ¼ pint salad oil, about 2 dessertspoons wine vinegar)
½ lb tomatoes
1 teaspoon tomato purée
dash of Tabasco sauce

To garnish
½ bunch of watercress

Method

Halve the eggs lengthways, remove the yolks and pound with the butter; keep the egg whites in a bowl of cold water until wanted. Chop the pimiento, rub it through a fine strainer and add to the egg yolk and butter mixture. Season and soften, if necessary, with about 1 teaspoon of mayonnaise.

Scald and skin tomatoes and slice half of them. Quarter the others, scoop out seeds and reserve; cut the flesh in fine strips.

Season the mayonnaise with the tomato purée and Tabasco sauce and thin, as necessary, with a little of the juice strained from the tomato seeds, to give a good coating consistency. Drain the egg whites and dry on absorbent paper, fill with the yolk and pimiento mixture and press halves back together.

Arrange eggs on a serving dish and coat each one with 1 tablespoon mayonnaise; place the sliced tomatoes around the eggs and put a spoonful of tomato strips on each egg. Garnish with watercress and serve with brown bread and butter.

Egg and beetroot salad

6 eggs (hard-boiled)
4 small, round cooked beetroots, or 1 lb jar of pickled baby beetroots
½ lb small new potatoes
3 spring onions
2 teaspoons caster sugar
1 teaspoon dry mustard
¼ teaspoon salt
black pepper (ground from mill)
1 tablespoon wine vinegar
1 tablespoon grated horseradish
3 tablespoons double cream
¼ pint boiled dressing, or mayonnaise

Method

Peel and slice the beetroots, scrape and cook the potatoes and chop the spring onions. Mix the sugar, mustard, salt and pepper with the vinegar, then stir in the horseradish and the cream.

If the potatoes are very small, leave them whole; otherwise quarter or slice them, mix while still warm with the horseradish cream and the chopped onion. Mix in the sliced beetroot and turn on to a serving dish; arrange the halved eggs on top and coat with the boiled dressing (or mayonnaise).

Veal and pepper salad

2 slices fillet of veal (about $\frac{1}{2}$ lb
  in all)
1 tablespoon olive oil
1 shallot (finely chopped)
1 teaspoon tomato purée
1 glass sherry ($2\frac{1}{2}$ fl oz)
4 oz button mushrooms
4 oz cooked ham (shredded)
2 green peppers (sliced)
French dressing
$\frac{1}{2}$ lb tomatoes (sliced)

Method
Sauté the slices of veal in the oil until golden on each side. Add the finely chopped shallot to the pan and continue cooking for 2-3 minutes, stir in the tomato purée, add the sherry and cover pan, then simmer for 5 minutes. Add the mushrooms and continue cooking a further 5 minutes. Leave to cool.

Cut the ham into shreds. Slice, blanch and refresh the peppers. Cut the veal into thick julienne strips and then mix all ingredients together (except tomatoes) with French dressing and put into serving dish. Garnish with tomato slices.

Veal salad

4 escalopes of veal
1 tablespoon olive oil
salt and pepper
1 glass golden sherry
$\frac{1}{2}$ lb new potatoes
4 tablespoons French dressing
8 pickled walnuts (sliced)
1 tablespoon mixed chopped
  herbs

For dressing
1 teaspoon paprika pepper
$\frac{1}{2}$ clove of garlic (crushed with
  $\frac{1}{4}$ teaspoon salt)
$\frac{1}{4}$ pint soured cream
caster sugar, or lemon juice

This salad can be made with cold roast veal left over from a previous meal.

Method
Heat the oil and brown the escalopes on each side, season, pour over the sherry, cover the pan and simmer gently for 8-10 minutes. Leave to cool.

Scrape and cook the potatoes, slice them and mix with the French dressing while still warm. Cut each escalope in 3-4 pieces, mix with the potatoes, walnuts and herbs and turn into a salad bowl or serving dish.

To make the dressing : mix the paprika with the crushed garlic and stir in the soured cream. Season to taste with salt, sugar or lemon juice, as liked. Spoon this dressing over the veal salad about 15 minutes before serving.

Salt beef salad

8-12 oz salted brisket of beef
(sliced)
4 large old potatoes
1 dessertspoon dry mustard
1 tablespoon demerara sugar
1 tablespoon malt vinegar
$\frac{1}{4}$ pint mayonnaise
1 dill cucumber (chopped)
1 lettuce heart (quartered)
2 eggs (hard-boiled)

Method

Shred the salt beef and boil the potatoes in their jackets. Mix the mustard and sugar with the vinegar and stir until dissolved. Peel the potatoes while hot and slice a layer into the serving dish, spread with a thin coating of mayonnaise and sprinkle with a little of the cucumber. Cover with a layer of salt beef and moisten with some of the mustard dressing; continue in this way until beef and potatoes are used.

Garnish the dish with the lettuce heart and the quartered hard-boiled eggs.

Chopping dill cucumber to add to the shredded salt beef salad

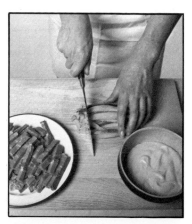

Beef salad

8-12 oz cold cooked beef
(preferably underdone)
1 teaspoon paprika pepper
½ teaspoon dry mustard
pepper
½ clove of garlic (crushed with
¼ teaspoon salt)
1 tablespoon red wine vinegar
3 tablespoons olive oil
1 dill cucumber
9 black olives
½ lb tomatoes
6 slices of French bread

Method
Cut the beef in ¼-inch slices and then in julienne strips. Mix the seasonings and garlic with the vinegar, then whisk in the oil. When this dressing is thick, pour it over the beef and leave to marinate while preparing the other ingredients.

Slice the cucumber; halve and stone the olives; scald, skin and quarter the tomatoes and scoop out the seeds.

Place the French bread in a serving dish and put a good spoonful of the beef and dressing on each slice. Arrange the sliced cucumber between every other portion of beef with the olives on the top and fill in with the quartered tomatoes.

Spiced ham and egg salad

12 eggs (hard-boiled)
1 lb sliced ham
1 teaspoon paprika pepper
salt and pepper
dash of Tabasco sauce
2 tablespoons red wine
vinegar
4 tablespoons tomato ketchup
6 tablespoons salad oil
3 tablespoons mango chutney
1 pinch of saffron (soaked in 2 tablespoons boiling water for about 30 minutes)
½ pint mayonnaise
1 lb long grain rice (boiled, drained and dried well)
watercress (to garnish)

This quantity serves 12 people.

Method
Mix the paprika, salt and pepper and Tabasco with the vinegar and stir in the tomato ketchup. Then add the oil, whisk well until the mixture thickens and taste for seasoning. If the mango chutney is rather coarse, cut the mango into thin strips; add to the dressing. Cut the ham into shreds and mix with the dressing.

Strain the saffron through a nylon strainer and beat the liquid into the mayonnaise. Taste the mayonnaise for seasoning and then mix into the rice. Arrange this rice on a serving dish. Cut the hard-boiled eggs in half and arrange on top of the rice. Spoon the spiced ham mixture over the eggs and garnish the dish with watercress.

Italian salad with noodles

1½ lb piece middle cut gammon
1 carrot (peeled)
1 onion (peeled)
8 oz green noodles (or tagliatelle)
½ lb firm white mushrooms
4 oz black olives (stoned)

For dressing
2 tablespoons red wine vinegar
salt and pepper
6 tablespoons olive oil
4 tablespoons piquant tomato
   sauce, ketchup or chutney
1 tablespoon chopped herbs

For garnish
½ lb tomatoes
½ pint mayonnaise
French mustard

This is just one of several
versions of Italian salad. The
main ingredient should be pasta
of some kind with a cut meat —
either veal or ham.

The following recipe is made
with green noodles or tagliatelle.
It is sufficient for 6-8 people
and would be suitable for a
supper party.

Method

Put the gammon in a saucepan,
cover with cold water, bring it
slowly to the boil and then skim
well. Add the carrot and onion to
flavour, cook for 1 hour and leave
to cool in the liquid.

Cook the pasta in plenty of
boiling salted water for about
12 minutes, drain and rinse with
cold water until shiny, then drain
again. Trim and wash the
mushrooms, slice thickly if large.

To prepare the dressing: mix
the vinegar with the seasoning
then whisk in the oil and all
the other ingredients.

Scald, skin and slice the
tomatoes. Cut the gammon into
finger-size pieces and put in
a bowl with the noodles, mushrooms and olives. Pour over
the dressing and mix carefully.
Put in a deep serving dish and
arrange the tomato slices round
the salad. Thin the mayonnaise
with a little boiling water, if
necessary, and flavour with a
touch of French mustard. Serve
this mayonnaise separately.

Pork salad

8-12 oz cold roast pork, or cold
  boiled salt pork
1 cup finely shredded white Dutch
  cabbage
2 tablespoons olive oil
2 tart dessert apples (peeled and
  sliced)
$\frac{1}{4}$ teaspoon salt
pepper
$\frac{1}{2}$ teaspoon French mustard
2 tablespoons cider
2 tablespoons double cream
1 tablespoon snipped chives, or
  chopped parsley

Method
Dice the cold pork. Put the
cabbage in a large bowl,
sprinkle with the olive oil and
turn it with 2 wooden spoons
until every shred is coated with
a film of oil, then add the sliced
apple.

Mix the seasonings and mustard with the cider and whisk in
the cream. Add the pork to the
cabbage, spoon the cider cream
dressing over them and turn
into a serving dish. Sprinkle with
chives or parsley.

Barossa chicken

$3\frac{1}{2}$ lb roasting chicken
$1\frac{1}{2}$-2 oz butter
1 wineglass white wine
1 lettuce (shredded)
4 oz almonds (blanched and
  split — see page 136)
2 tablespoons olive oil
$\frac{1}{2}$ lb muscat grapes
squeeze of lemon juice
salt and pepper

For dressing
1 wineglass white wine
juice of $\frac{1}{2}$ lemon
about $\frac{1}{4}$ pint olive oil
1 tablespoon mixed chopped herbs
  (parsley, mint and chives)

This recipe was called Barossa
after the name of an Australian
vineyard.

Method
Set oven at 400°F or Mark 6.
Roast the chicken for about 1
hour with the butter and white
wine. Reserve any juice from
roasting chicken. Leave chicken
to get quite cold, then joint it
and arrange on the shredded
lettuce on a serving dish.

Fry the almonds in the oil
until brown, drain and salt them
lightly. Peel and pip the grapes,
put them in a small basin or tea
cup, sprinkle with a little lemon
juice to prevent discolouration,
cover with greaseproof paper.

To make the dressing : boil
the wine to reduce it to half
quantity, then take it off heat.
Mix the wine with the rest of the
dressing ingredients, seasoning
and juice reserved from roasting
the chicken, well skimmed of
any fat. Add the grapes, and
spoon this dressing over the
chicken; then scatter over the
almonds.

Chicken and cherry salad

3 lb roasting chicken
salt and pepper
2 oz butter
$\frac{1}{2}$ pint stock (made from the
   giblets — see page 139)
1 tablespoon wine vinegar
4 tablespoons oil
1 tablespoon mixed chopped fresh
   herbs (parsley, mint and thyme)
1 lb red cherries (stoned)
tarragon cream dressing
2 lettuce hearts

Method

Set oven at 400°F or Mark 6. Season and rub $\frac{1}{2}$ oz butter inside chicken, rub the remaining butter over it and then 'French roast' (see page 138), using half the stock, in the preset oven for about 1 hour; turn and baste from time to time.

When cooked and evenly browned remove from pan, pour in the remaining stock, boil it up well, strain and reserve.

Carve chicken and arrange meat round a serving dish. Mix vinegar with salt and pepper and whisk in oil. Remove fat from the chicken juices and add these with the herbs to the oil and vinegar. Taste this dressing for seasoning and spoon it over the chicken.

Mix the cherries with the tarragon dressing. Arrange the chicken on the serving dish. Split the lettuce hearts and fill with the cherry mixture. Place in centre of the chicken.

'French roast' chicken and cherries in tarragon cream dressing

Chicken salad milanaise

3-4 lb roasting chicken
2 oz butter
pinch of marjoram
salt and pepper
1 wineglass dry vermouth
$\frac{1}{2}$ pint jellied chicken stock (see page 139)
4 oz cooked ham
4 oz cooked tongue

For salad
8 oz cut macaroni
$\frac{1}{2}$ lb button mushrooms (washed and trimmed)
juice of $\frac{1}{4}$ lemon
2 tablespoons olive oil
salt and pepper
$\frac{1}{4}$ pint mayonnaise

For garnish
1 bunch of watercress

This quantity serves 10-12 people.

Method
Set the oven at 400°F or Mark 6.

Put $\frac{1}{2}$ oz of the butter, the marjoram and seasoning inside the chicken, truss bird neatly and rub the remaining butter over it. Place bird in a roasting tin, pour round vermouth, cover breast with a buttered paper and put in the pre-set oven. Baste bird after 20 minutes, remove paper and turn chicken on its side; continue to baste it every 20 minutes. When the vermouth has evaporated and the butter begins to brown, add a little of the jellied stock. Turn the bird as it browns and finish the cooking with the breast uppermost. (Total cooking time, about 1-1$\frac{1}{2}$ hours.)

Remove the bird from the roasting tin and leave to cool. Tip the remaining stock into the roasting tin, bring to the boil and scrape down sediment from the sides of the pan. Strain this and leave to cool.

To prepare the salad: cook the macaroni in boiling salted water until just tender (about 12-15 minutes), drain and rinse under the cold tap until very shiny. Cut the mushrooms in thick slices, put in a pan with the lemon juice and cook very quickly for 1 minute only, turn out on to a plate to cool. Sprinkle the mushrooms with the oil, turning them in it carefully until completely coated, then season. Mix the mayonnaise into the macaroni, add the mushrooms and turn the salad carefully into the serving dish. Carve the chicken, cutting the flesh in neat, even-size pieces (removing the bones) and arrange on top of the salad.

Cut the ham and tongue into julienne strips. Remove all traces of fat from the cooking liquor from the chicken (this is easy if it is cold) and mix the remainder with the strips of ham and tongue.

Watchpoint Ham soon loses its pink colour if exposed to the air, so if you shred the ham and tongue during your preparation time, keep meat in a small basin covered with a piece of wet greaseproof paper.

Spoon the ham and tongue over the chicken and garnish with the watercress.

Chicken mayonnaise

1 roasting, or boiling, chicken
(4-5 lb)
root vegetables (to flavour) —
sliced
bouquet garni
6-8 peppercorns
1 teaspoon salt
$\frac{1}{2}$-$\frac{3}{4}$ pint mayonnaise
salt and pepper
lemon juice
strips of pimiento (to decorate)

This recipe serves 6 people.

Method

Place chicken in a large pan, add the root vegetables, bouquet garni, peppercorns and salt. Pour on enough cold water to come level with the top of the chicken legs (if using a boiling chicken, water should cover the bird completely). Cover with a piece of foil or greaseproof paper and the lid and set pan on a low heat. After it has reached boiling point, simmer for $1\frac{1}{4}$-$1\frac{1}{2}$ hours, longer for a boiling fowl. Draw pan aside and cool chicken in the liquid.

When chicken is cold, take it out of the liquid, remove all skin and cut the meat from the carcass. Shred white and dark meat, keeping them separate; arrange on a large tray or dish.

Season the mayonnaise well and sharpen it, if necessary, with a few drops of lemon juice. Spoon a good half of this over the chicken, lifting the pieces lightly with a fork to allow the mayonnaise to penetrate. Set aside.

When ready to serve, arrange the chicken in a serving dish in layers of white and dark meat. Thin the rest of the mayonnaise, if necessary, and use it to coat the chicken. Decorate with strips of pimiento. Serve a rice salad (see page 106) separately.

Chicken and pineapple salad

1 large boiling fowl, or (if preferred)
   2 4-lb roasting chickens
2 fresh pineapples
salt
pepper (ground from mill)
1 onion (quartered)
1 carrot (quartered)
bouquet garni
1 teaspoon caster sugar
2 tablespoons white wine vinegar
6 tablespoons salad oil
1 tablespoon chopped parsley
1 tablespoon chopped mint
1 bunch of watercress (to garnish)

This quantity serves 12 people. This dish should be completed at least 2 hours before serving to give the chicken meat a chance to absorb the flavour of the pineapple dressing.

Method

Put the chicken in a large saucepan with enough water to cover. (If using roasting chickens, water should only cover legs and thighs.) Bring slowly to the boil, add the seasoning, vegetables and bouquet garni; simmer gently until quite tender. Allow about $1\frac{1}{2}$ - 2 hours for boiling fowl but only 50- 60 minutes for roasting chicken. Leave to cool in the liquid.

Peel and slice the pineapples (see page 91), cut each slice in half and stamp out the core with a small plain cutter. Mix salt, pepper and sugar with the vinegar and whisk in the oil. Remove the skin from the chicken, cut the meat into even-size pieces and arrange on a serving dish.

Cover the chicken with the sliced pineapple, add the herbs to the dressing, whisk again and spoon over the pineapple and chicken. Garnish with watercress just before serving.

Stuffed spring chickens in aspic

7 double poussins
¾-1 lb veal, or pork (minced)
1 small onion (finely chopped)
1 oz butter
1 dessertspoon chopped thyme and parsley
½ pint measure (3 oz) of fresh breadcrumbs
1 small egg (beaten)
salt and pepper

To roast
4-6 oz butter
1 pint strong stock (made from the giblets — see page 139)

This quantity serves 12.

Method

Ask your butcher to partially bone out the poussins, leaving the leg and breast bones; season cut surface. Soften the onion in the butter, cool, then add to minced veal (or pork) with herbs and crumbs. Mix well, bind with egg and season well. Divide this farce equally between the poussins, reshape them, secure with poultry pins and truss. Thickly butter grease-proof paper, tuck round the poussins, and pour enough stock into the roasting tin just to cover bottom. Roast at 400°F or Mark 6 for 35-40 minutes, basting well and turning birds 2 or 3 times; add more stock to the tin if necessary.

Take up birds, deglaze tin with stock and pour off into bowl. Leave to get cold. When poussins are cold remove strings, split and trim. Arrange poussins down long serving dish.

Scoop off butter from the gravy and spoon the jelly over the chicken. Garnish dish with watercress and 'croûtes' of aspic jelly. Serve with appropriate salads.

Chicken and avocado salad

3 lb roasting chicken
1 onion (peeled)
1 carrot (peeled)
bouquet garni
1 teaspoon salt
6 peppercorns
1 head of celery
4 oz shelled walnuts
½ pint boiled dressing, or mayonnaise
2 avocado pears (peeled, stoned and quartered)
4 tablespoons French dressing
1 tablespoon chopped parsley and chives (mixed)
1 teaspoon chopped gherkin

Method

Put the chicken in a pot and cover with hot water. Add the onion, carrot, bouquet garni and seasoning and simmer gently for about 1 hour or until tender. Leave to cool in the liquid.

Wash and trim the celery and cut in sticks 1-1½ inches in length; soak in ice-cold water for about 1 hour, then drain and dry. Remove the skin and bones from the chicken, cut the flesh into neat finger-size pieces and mix with the celery and walnuts; pour the boiled dressing (or mayonnaise) over them and toss to coat well. Turn chicken salad on to a serving dish and surround with avocado pears. Mix the French dressing with the herbs and gherkin and spoon at once over the avocados.

Side salads

This is where salads come truly into their own, as accompaniments to grander dishes. Whether you are serving hot or cold meat, poultry or fish, you can serve a salad either instead of, or as well as, conventional vegetables.

In winter, when the choice of fresh green vegetables becomes limited you may be particularly glad to use salads as a source of variety. Take your pick from hard white cabbage, carrots, chicory, curly endive and celery, served raw with a suitable dressing. Or cook your vegetables and then serve them cold — leeks, onions, beetroot, celeriac, jerusalem artichokes, potatoes and cauliflower all lend themselves to this treatment.

Choose your vegetables and fruit carefully to complement the flavours in the main dish, and use only vegetables that are in the best condition. Dress them carefully with a delicate dressing, just before serving, and you will get full marks for imaginative meal planning.

Mushroom and Gruyère salad

½ lb white button mushrooms
olive oil (to sauté)
French dressing (to moisten)
1 shallot (finely chopped)
6 oz broad beans (weighed when shelled)
6 oz Gruyère cheese
lettuce, or watercress

Method
Wash and wipe mushrooms, sauté quickly in a little olive oil. Set aside, and moisten with French dressing while still hot. Add the shallot. Leave to get cold. Cook beans and remove the outer jackets, set aside. Cut the Gruyère into match-size pieces and add to the mushrooms with the broad beans. Add more dressing if necessary, and season well. Arrange the salad on a dish surrounded with well-washed lettuce or watercress.

Celery sticks

1 large head of celery
4 oz cream cheese
1-2 tablespoons top of milk
salt
pepper (ground from mill)
paprika pepper

Method
Wash celery thoroughly and cut sticks into 3-inch lengths. Soften cheese with top of the milk, add seasoning and mix well. Fill celery sticks with cheese mixture and dust with paprika pepper.

Roquefort and walnut salad

2 lettuces (hearts only)
3 slices of white bread
1½ oz Roquefort, or other blue cheese (crushed)
6 large walnuts, or 12 half-kernels
8 tablespoons French dressing

Method
Wash and dry lettuces, chill until crisp. Cut crusts from bread and toast until golden-brown. When cold cut each slice into four and spread with the crushed Roquefort. Shell walnuts and, if wished, blanch kernels to remove skins. Make a French dressing.

Just before serving mix lettuce, walnuts and Roquefort 'toasts' with the dressing.

Butter bean and anchovy salad

½ lb butter beans (soaked and pre-cooked — see page 137)
12 anchovy fillets
French dressing (made with 2 tablespoons red wine vinegar to 3 tablespoons salad oil, salt, pepper and a little sugar)
1 shallot (finely chopped)
2 tablespoons double cream
1 tablespoon chopped chives

Method
Leave the beans to cool in the cooking liquor, then drain. Soak anchovy fillets in a little milk for about 15 minutes, then drain. Prepare French dressing, add the shallot and the cream. Cut anchovies into ½-inch strips, add to dressing and spoon over the beans. Sprinkle with chives.

This salad is good with lamb.

Breton salad

2 medium-size carrots (diced)
1 turnip (diced)
4 oz French beans (cut in diamonds)
2 tablespoons French dressing
3 potatoes (about 6-8 oz)

For mock mayonnaise
$\frac{1}{2}$ teaspoon dry mustard
$\frac{1}{2}$ teaspoon caster sugar
$\frac{1}{4}$ teaspoon salt
$\frac{1}{4}$ teaspoon pepper
5 tablespoons evaporated milk
5 tablespoons salad oil
2 dessertspoons vinegar

To garnish
1 egg (hard-boiled)
1 tablespoon mixed chopped herbs

A garnish of hard-boiled eggs and herbs gives an attractive finish

Method
To prepare mock mayonnaise: place the mustard, sugar and seasoning in a small basin and mix smoothly with the milk. Add the oil gradually, whisking briskly all the time. Whisk in the vinegar, which forms an emulsion with the oil and thickens the dressing.

Cook the carrot, turnip and beans separately until tender, then mix them, while still hot, with the French dressing. Boil the potatoes in their skins, skin and dice them and add to the other vegetables. Add sufficient mock mayonnaise dressing to bind vegetables together.

Pile the mixture in a salad bowl, garnish with quarters of hard-boiled egg and sprinkle over the herbs.

Serve with cold ham, chicken or veal.

Green salad with fresh pineapple

1 lettuce
1 small fresh pineapple
1 tablespoon caster sugar

For French dressing
2 tablespoons wine vinegar
salt
pepper (ground from mill)
6 tablespoons salad oil
1 teaspoon parsley (chopped) —
  optional

To peel and cut fresh pineapple :
slice bottom off with a serrated-edge knife, hold the pineapple firmly and cut downwards between 'eyes' at an angle of about 45° with a sharp, stainless steel knife. These eyes should then come out easily in strips. Now remove the top, slice the flesh and remove core with a grapefruit knife. This method of peeling and coring will avoid waste.

Method
Cut the skin from the pineapple, slice the flesh and discard the core. Sprinkle with sugar. Leave for at least 30 minutes.

Wash lettuce, drain, wrap in a clean tea towel or a paper towel, then leave in the refrigerator to get really crisp. If you haven't a refrigerator, leave preparation of the lettuce until the last minute or it will become soft and limp.

Prepare French dressing and pour a little over the pineapple.

Just before serving, put lettuce leaves in a salad bowl and toss them in enough dressing to coat each leaf (beat remainder of dressing again just before using). Add pineapple to the lettuce, sprinkle with parsley and serve at once.

Orange and pineapple salad

3 large seedless oranges
1 medium-size pineapple
French dressing (made with 2 table-
    spoons white wine vinegar, 4 table-
    spoons olive oil, squeeze of lemon
    juice, pepper and salt, caster
    sugar to taste)
curly endive, or 1 small lettuce

For preference use fresh pineapple — the small Cape pineapples are good.

Method
Slice away peel and remove
pith from the oranges and cut
the flesh into segments with
a sharp knife. Peel and core the
pineapple (see page 91) and cut
into pieces, the same size as
the orange sections if possible.
Mix with French dressing.
　　Arrange the curly endive or
lettuce on individual plates or
in a bowl and spoon the fruit
into the centre. Chill salad
before serving.

Chicory and orange salad

1 lb chicory
3 oranges
2 large carrots
French dressing

Method
Wash chicory, trim away stalk,
separate leaves or cut into
pieces. Remove peel and skin
from oranges with a sharp knife,
then cut into segments and
discard any pips. Shred the
carrot into fine julienne strips
(about $1\frac{1}{2}$ -2 inches long). Mix
ingredients together and toss in
French dressing.

Orange and brazil nut salad

4 large oranges
2-3 oz brazil nuts (shelled)
1 crisp lettuce, or 1 curly endive

For dressing
French dressing
1 shallot (finely chopped)
1 dessertspoon chopped parsley

Method
Peel the oranges, then slice
them into thin rounds. Grate
nuts with a cheese grater. Wash
and dry lettuce or endive.
　　Place lettuce (or endive) in a
salad bowl with orange slices
on top ; scatter with nuts.
　　Spoon over French dressing,
mixed with shallot and parsley.
Chill before serving.
　　If preferred, the nuts may be
left whole, soaked for an hour,
then thinly sliced lengthwise.

Orange salad

3 seedless oranges
freshly pared rind of $\frac{1}{2}$ orange
French dressing (made with 1-2
    tablespoons white, or red, wine
    vinegar, 3-4 tablespoons olive oil
    and seasoning)

Method
First pare off the rind of half an
orange, shred, blanch and
drain. Set aside. Then slice
away the peel and pith from the
oranges and cut into sections.
Arrange these in a small dish.
Prepare a well-seasoned French
dressing from the oil and vinegar and spoon this over. Scatter
over the blanched peel. Chill
slightly before serving.

Tomato and orange salad

$\frac{1}{2}$ lb tomatoes
1 teaspoon caster sugar
3 oranges
French dressing
grated orange rind (blanched)

Method
Scald, skin and thinly slice the tomatoes and place them in a dish; scatter over the caster sugar.

Cut away the peel and remove the pith from the oranges, then slice or divide them into sections. Place oranges in the dish with the tomatoes and moisten with the French dressing. Finish with a sprinkling of blanched orange rind.

Serve with cold ham and hot, or cold, roast duck.

Carrot and raisin salad

$1\frac{1}{2}$ lb carrots
$\frac{1}{2}$ lb raisins
juice of 2 large oranges
French dressing (made with 2 table-spoons vinegar, salt, pepper from mill, 6 tablespoons salad oil)

Method
Wash the raisins in hot water, cover with the strained orange juice and leave to soak until well plumped. Peel the carrots and coarsely grate them. Mix grated carrots with the raisins and moisten with the French dressing.

Fennel and lemon salad

2-3 heads of fennel (according to size)
2 ripe thin-skinned lemons

For dressing
juice of extra $\frac{1}{2}$ lemon (see method)
3 tablespoons oil
salt and pepper
caster sugar (to taste)
1 tablespoon roughly chopped parsley

Florence fennel (finocchio) makes an excellent salad, clean and fresh tasting. If the aniseed flavour is a little strong for some tastes, qualify it with other salad vegetables, such as celery and chicory. This salad goes well with wild duck or other rich meat.

Method
Slice fennel finely and put into a bowl. Pare 2-3 strips of rind from 1 lemon and cut into shreds, then blanch, drain and refresh it and set aside. Slice away peel and white pith from both lemons and cut out the flesh from between membranes with a sharp knife, holding the lemon in one hand so that eventually only the membranes are left in your hand. Add lemon segments to the fennel.

To make dressing: squeeze the membranes left from the two lemons to get out any juice and, if necessary, make up to a good tablespoon with some of the juice from the extra $\frac{1}{2}$ lemon. Beat in the oil and season well. Make the dressing rather sweet, especially if the lemons are not really ripe. Add it to the salad with the parsley. Toss well and scatter with the blanched lemon rind.

93

Grape, melon and mint salad

1 honeydew, or cantaloup, melon
$\frac{1}{2}$-$\frac{3}{4}$ lb green grapes
about 6 sprigs of young mint
French dressing (made with 2 table-
    spoons white wine vinegar, 4
    tablespoons olive oil, squeeze of
    lemon juice, salt, pepper and
    caster sugar to taste)

To serve with roast chicken.

Method
Cut the melon in half, scrape away the seeds carefully, then scoop out the flesh into balls with a round vegetable cutter (potato scoop), or a teaspoon. Peel and pip the grapes.
Watchpoint Peel the grapes before flicking out the seeds with the point of a knife or potato peeler. (To peel them easily, dip the bunch for a few seconds into boiling water.)

Mix ingredients together for the dressing and season well to taste. Cut the scraped out melon rind into slices or leave in 2 halves and arrange on individual plates or in a dish. Mix the melon balls, grapes and mint together with the dressing, then spoon into the melon shells or on to individual slices. Chill a little before serving.

Peach and ginger salad

1 lettuce heart
3 fresh peaches
3 tablespoons preserved ginger (sliced)
salt
pepper (ground from mill)
juice of $\frac{1}{2}$ lemon
1 tablespoon ginger syrup
2 tablespoons olive oil
chopped parsley (to finish)

Method
Trim and wash the lettuce, remove the heart only and dry lettuce thoroughly in a cloth or absorbent kitchen paper, then open it out.

Scald, skin and slice the peaches (after removing the stones), mix with the ginger and spoon into the centre of the lettuce. Arrange this on a serving dish.

Mix the seasoning with the lemon juice and ginger syrup and whisk in the oil until the mixture thickens. Spoon this over the fruit and dust with a little chopped parsley.

Chicory, apple and walnut salad

1 lb chicory
2 dessert apples (preferably
  Cox's Orange Pippins)
2 oz walnuts (shelled)

For dressing
1 tablespoon wine vinegar
salt, pepper and caster sugar (to
  taste)
2 tablespoons salad oil
2 tablespoons single cream

Method
Wipe the chicory, remove any damaged leaves, cut across in thick slices and place in a salad bowl. Cut apples in four, remove core, slice and put into bowl without peeling. Add walnuts and mix well.

Prepare the dressing by mixing the vinegar with the seasonings in a bowl and whisking in the oil and cream.

Pour dressing over salad and mix well. Chill.

Potato, celery and apple salad

$\frac{3}{4}$ lb potatoes
1 head of celery
1 large tart apple
$\frac{1}{4}$ pint lemon cream dressing

Method
Scrub the potatoes and cook in their skins in boiling, salted water until tender. Slice celery, prepare lemon cream dressing. Now peel and slice potatoes and apple, add to celery and moisten with some dressing. Serve coated with remaining lemon cream dressing.

Celery, apple and walnut salad

1 large head of celery
2 Cox's apples
handful of walnut kernels (preferably fresh ones)
French dressing
parsley (chopped) — to garnish

Method
Trim and wash celery. Cut into 2-inch lengths, then cut downwards into sticks. Leave in ice-cold water to crisp for 30 minutes, then drain and dry thoroughly. Put into a bowl with apples (cored and sliced but not peeled) and the walnut kernels (slightly broken). Mix with enough French dressing to moisten well. Leave to stand, covered, for 30-60 minutes and scatter with chopped parsley just before serving.

Corn salad, with beetroot and apple

large bunch of corn salad (lamb's
   lettuce)
2 medium-size beetroots
   (cooked and sliced)
1 large tart apple (peeled, cored
   and sliced)
French dressing

Or substitute for corn salad
1 head of celery (washed)
1 Spanish onion (peeled)
parsley or walnuts (chopped) for
   garnish

Corn salad (or lamb's lettuce)
is rarely seen in the shops. However, it is easy to grow and is
unharmed by frost. Though
dull eaten alone, it is excellent
in a mixed salad.

Method
Wash corn salad well and dry
thoroughly. Put corn salad,
sliced beetroot and apple in a
large bowl, and toss in the
French dressing.

If using celery and onion
rings instead of corn salad, cut
washed celery into short sticks,
slice onion and push out into
rings. Blanch rings by plunging
into boiling water for 2-3 minutes,
then drain and refresh (rinse in
cold water and drain again).
Dress as above, and leave
covered for 2-3 hours after
adding beetroot and apple.
Scatter chopped parsley or
walnuts over this salad before
serving.

Coleslaw and fruit salad

½ white drumhead cabbage
olive oil (to moisten)
salt
black pepper (ground from mill)
½ lb white grapes
½ lb Colmar grapes
2 Cox's apples
2 oranges
2 clementine oranges
little caster sugar (for dusting)
lemon juice or white wine
  vinegar

The Colmar grape is a sweet variety of black grape.

Coleslaw and fruit — an unusual mixture of cabbage and fresh grapes, apples and oranges

Method
Trim the cabbage and wipe well but keep dry. Shred very finely and then dress with enough olive oil to moisten, season with salt and pepper, cover and put in the refrigerator.

Prepare the fruit: peel grapes and remove pips. Peel and core apples and cut into dice. Peel oranges and clementines and cut into segments, removing membranes. Dust fruits with caster sugar and sprinkle with the lemon juice or vinegar; cover dish and keep in the refrigerator. Just before serving, mix the cabbage and fruits together and pile into a large salad bowl.

Green salad

lettuce, or selection of salad greens
(see method)
French dressing
garlic (optional)
chopped mixed herbs (eg. thyme,
chives, mint and parsley)

A green salad mixed with a French dressing and liberally sprinkled with chopped herbs and parsley is a classic accompaniment to French roast chicken and is often served with, or after, a main course, particularly if there are no green vegetables with the dish.

Green salads can be of plain lettuce — cabbage, cos, Webb's or Iceberg, depending on the season — or be a mixture of salad greens, such as watercress, sliced cucumber and spring onions. Chicory can also be added in season, but tomato and beetroot (which normally go into an English salad) are best served separately.

Method

Preparation of the salad greens is of great importance. Lettuce leaves should be carefully detached and the outside coarse ones discarded. A fruit or stainless steel knife (not a carbon knife) may be used to trim the bottom stalk, or to quarter the hearts if using them for garnish. If the leaves are too large, pull rather than cut them apart. Wash them well, then swing dry in a salad basket or clean muslin cloth. Make sure this is thoroughly done. If lettuce is at all limp, put it into the refrigerator (in the salad drawer or hydrator) until crisp. Watercress should be well

rinsed in the bunch under the cold tap, then shaken to get rid of the moisture. Carefully pick over and remove some of the stalk, but if this is clean (ie. free from any little hairs) do not discard. These stalks can be snipped into little pieces with scissors and used with chopped herbs, or scattered over vegetable soups, or for a savoury butter. They have a pleasant, slightly peppery taste.

Garlic may be used to flavour, but use it cautiously in a green salad. Either rub the bowl with a peeled clove, or better still, rub a clove well over a crust of French or ordinary bread. Having put the salad into the bowl, bury this chapon, as it is called, among the leaves (not forgetting to remove it before serving the salad at the table).

A green salad should be dressed at the last moment, otherwise the leaves will wilt and be unappetising. For a large amount of salad, you will find it easier to mix with its dressing in a really big bowl, and then to transfer it to your salad bowl.

There is, however, a way of dressing the salad where the leaves remain crisp for slightly longer. Sprinkle in enough oil on its own, tossing the leaves all the time to make them glisten. Mix the vinegar (a third of the quantity of oil used) and seasoning together, and sprinkle over the bowl. For a stronger flavour crush garlic with a little salt and add to this dressing. Stir once or twice before serving the salad, so that the dressing is evenly distributed. Before serving, sprinkle with chopped herbs and parsley.

Salad vegetables and herbs, from left to right, front : cucumber, green pepper, cabbage lettuce, chicory (English), cos lettuce. Behind ; watercress, thyme, chives, mint, parsley, garlic, endive (English), Webb's Wonder lettuce in basket

Beetroot jelly salad

1 jar, or small can, whole beetroots
juice from 1 medium-size can raspberries
salt and pepper
1 dessertspoon red wine vinegar
1 oz gelatine

Ring mould (1-1¼ pints capacity)

Method
Drain the liquid from the canned beetroots and raspberries. Mix these liquids together, season and sharpen very slightly with the wine vinegar. Measure out 1½ pints of liquid, making it up with water if necessary. Add gelatine to this and dissolve it over gentle heat (it is not essential to soak gelatine first in this recipe).

Cut the beetroot into fine slices, or grate it, and arrange in wet mould. Pour over the cool liquid and leave to set. Turn out and serve with cold roast beef and horseradish cream.

Beetroot, celeriac and walnut salad

1 large beetroot (cooked and sliced)
1 large celeriac root
2 tablespoons walnut kernels (coarsely chopped)
½ pint thick mayonnaise

Fluted cutter

Method
Slice beetroot and cut into crescents with fluted cutter. Wash, peel and slice celeriac, cut across into julienne strips (about 1½-2 inches long). Blanch by plunging into pan of boiling water until barely tender (4-5 minutes), then drain strips thoroughly.

Lightly brown chopped walnuts in a medium oven for a few minutes or under the grill. Put celeriac into a salad bowl and mix in 2 tablespoons of mayonnaise with a little boiling water. Spoon over rest of mayonnaise and surround with crescents of beetroot. Scatter walnuts over the top. Serve at once.

Beetroot with golden swede

1½ lb cooked beetroots
1 swede
French dressing (made with 2 table-
    spoons vinegar, salt, pepper
    from mill, 3 tablespoons salad oil)
1 small carton (2½ fl oz) double
    cream
1 tablespoon snipped chives
salt
pepper (ground from mill)

This quantity serves 12 people.

Method
Grate the beetroots and mix with the French dressing. Grate the raw swede and mix with the cream and chives; season. Arrange the beetroot round the edge of a large salad bowl and pile the swede in the centre.

Salade de saison

1 Webb's lettuce
1 avocado pear

For dressing
1 tablespoon white wine vinegar
salt and pepper
2 tablespoons salad oil
poppy seeds

Method
Wash and dry the lettuce very well and break into bite-size pieces. This is best done with the fingers. Prepare the dressing in the usual way, adding a few poppy seeds when the dressing is emulsified. Pour dressing over the lettuce and mix well. Peel the avocado, cut into thin slices and add to the lettuce. Toss once again, but avoid breaking the avocado. Tip into a large salad bowl.

Polish potato salad

1½ lb small new potatoes
2 tablespoons white wine
1 small beetroot
1 tablespoon finely grated
    horseradish
3 tablespoons mayonnaise
½ teaspoon caster sugar
pinch of dry mustard
salt and pepper
2 fl oz plain yoghourt

Method
Cook potatoes in their skins until tender, then skin while still hot and sprinkle with the white wine. Allow to cool.

Grate the beetroot very finely, mix with the horseradish and add to the mayonnaise. Mix sugar, mustard and seasoning together with the yoghourt and add this to the beetroot mixture. Spoon this dressing over the potatoes and serve.

Potato mayonnaise

1-1½ lb new potatoes
3-4 tablespoons French dressing
salt and pepper
¼ pint thick mayonnaise

To garnish
6 pickled walnuts
paprika pepper (optional)

Method
Scrub the potatoes and cook in their skins in boiling salted water until tender. Drain and dry, peel while still hot and cut in thick slices if the potatoes are large but keep whole if really small. Put in a bowl and moisten at once with the French dressing; season, cover and leave until cold.

When ready to serve, take 2 tablespoons of the mayonnaise, mix in carefully and turn potatoes into a dish. Thin the remaining mayonnaise with 1 dessertspoon of boiling water and spoon over the salad. Slice the pickled walnuts and arrange around the dish. Sprinkle the top with paprika, if you like this pungent, sweet spice.

Spicy potato salad

6 lb even-size old potatoes
½ lb streaky bacon
2 tablespoons malt vinegar
English mustard (dry)
1 jar of green pepper relish
¾ pint mayonnaise
1 tablespoon celery seeds

Method
Boil the potatoes in their skins until tender, then peel while hot. Meanwhile, fry the bacon until brown and crisp, remove it from the pan with a draining spoon, put in a bowl and crumble with a fork. Take the frying pan off the heat, add the vinegar, then pour off liquid into a small basin.

Thinly slice enough potato to make a layer in the serving dish, sprinkle with ¼ teaspoon of the mustard and 1 tablespoon of the relish, then cover with a layer of crumbled bacon with a little of the bacon fat, followed by a layer of mayonnaise and a sprinkling of celery seeds. Continue layering the potatoes in this way and finish with mayonnaise.

Tourangelle

¾ lb new potatoes
½ lb French beans
1 large tart apple (peeled and
   sliced)

For lemon cream dressing
¼ pint double cream
¼ pint mayonnaise
juice and grated rind of ½ lemon
salt and pepper
mustard

There are two types of salad
tourangelle. One is made with
new potatoes and French beans,
the other is more of a winter
salad and uses celery instead of
beans. This may be either stem
celery cut into short lengths or
the root celeriac. The method is
exactly the same.

Method
Scrub the potatoes and boil
them in their skins. Trim the
beans and cut them diagonally
into 1-inch long pieces, boil in
salted water until tender. Drain
and refresh.

   To prepare the dressing; stir
the cream into the mayonnaise,
gradually adding the grated rind
and lemon juice. Season well
and add a little boiling water, if
necessary, as the dressing
should not be too thick.

   Peel potatoes and cut into
thick julienne strips. Add the
bean and apple slices, moisten
with some of the dressing.
Arrange the salad in a dish and
coat with the rest of the lemon
cream dressing.

Lentil salad

6 oz Egyptian lentils (soaked in
   water overnight)
1 onion (stuck with clove)
1 carrot (cut in rounds)
salt
bouquet garni
stock (optional)
1 clove of garlic (crushed with
   ½ teaspoon salt)
4-6 tablespoons French dressing
pepper (ground from mill)
6-8 pickling onions
½ lb tomatoes
1 head of celery
1 lemon

This salad can be served with
cold roast chicken and game.

Method
Drain soaked lentils and cook
in plenty of slightly salted water
(brought slowly to the boil) with
onion, carrot and bouquet garni.
Simmer until tender and drain.
Remove bouquet garni and sieve
lentil mixture ; lighten with stock
if it is too thick and allow to
cool. Add the crushed garlic and
French dressing to the purée
and season very well, adding
plenty of ground black pepper.

   Slice the pickling onions,
scald and skin the tomatoes,
remove the core at the top,
squeeze out the seeds and chop
tomatoes roughly. Mix the pickling onions and tomatoes into
purée and pile into a serving
dish. Surround with curled
celery and lemon quarters.

Lyonnaise salad

4 large potatoes (1-1½ lb)
1 large onion (finely sliced)
2 tablespoons olive oil
4 tablespoons French dressing
1 dill cucumber (sliced)
1 tablespoon chopped parsley

Method
Boil the potatoes in their skins. Meanwhile cook the onion slowly in the oil until it is brown and crisp. Skin and slice potatoes.

Layer potato slices in a salad bowl with the cooked onion. Mix the French dressing with the dill cucumber and parsley and spoon it over the potatoes.

Serve with either hot or cold roast beef or lamb.

Sweetcorn salad

1 large can of sweetcorn kernels
1 green pepper (shredded and blanched)
4 tomatoes (skinned and quartered)
French dressing (to moisten)

Method
Drain the sweetcorn kernels well before mixing them with the prepared green pepper and tomatoes. Toss in enough French dressing to moisten well. If preferred, reserve the tomatoes, after dressing them separately, and place round the edge of the salad bowl.

Cabbage salad

white Dutch cabbage (very finely shredded)
3 tablespoons salad oil
black pepper (ground from mill)
1 tablespoon white wine vinegar

These drumhead cabbages are very tightly packed and a medium-size one generally weighs about 3 lb. You will find that this will serve at least 12 people.

Method
Remove the outside leaves of the cabbage, cut in four and remove the core. Shred the cabbage very finely, put in a large bowl with a few ice cubes and leave in a cool place for at least 1 hour. This will make the cabbage very crisp.

At the end of this time, drain away any liquid and sprinkle over salad oil. Keep turning the cabbage with 2 wooden spoons until every shred of cabbage is coated with oil, adding more oil if necessary. Now season and toss again to mix well.

The salad is now ready for the vinegar which is added in the proportion of 1 tablespoon vinegar to the 3 tablespoons salad oil already used. With this method the cabbage salad can be mixed with oil in the early morning for an evening party without losing its crisp texture. Add vinegar at last moment, toss again.

Vancouver salad

1 bunch of spring onions
2 green peppers
1 lb tomatoes (scalded and
   skinned)
1 teaspoon wine vinegar
salt and pepper
caster sugar
dry mustard
4 tablespoons mayonnaise
1 teaspoon French mustard
4 tablespoons soured cream

Method
Trim and wash the spring onions, removing most of the green part, and then chop. Slice the green peppers very thinly, removing the core and seeds, and blanch in boiling water for 1 minute; drain and refresh. Cut the tomatoes in wedges. Put onions, peppers and tomatoes in a salad bowl.

Mix the vinegar, salt, pepper, sugar and dry mustard together, then add them to the mayonnaise. Stir the French mustard into the cream, fold this into the mayonnaise and then mix into the vegetables. Cover and chill for 2 hours before serving.

Serve with grilled salmon.

Kachoomber

2 onions (chopped)
2 tomatoes (skinned and
   chopped)
1 green chilli (seeds removed
   and flesh chopped)
1 spray of green coriander
   leaves (chopped)
salt
vinegar
sugar

Method
Mix all ingredients together, adding the salt, vinegar and sugar to taste. This salad may be served with all curries.

Cauliflower with mustard mayonnaise

1 large cauliflower
1 carrot (grated)
½ pint mayonnaise
1 rounded teaspoon French
   mustard
salt and pepper
little creamy milk, or single
   cream (optional)
paprika pepper

Method
Wash cauliflower, break into sprigs and cook in boiling, salted water until barely tender (about 10 minutes). Drain and refresh. Dry sprigs thoroughly in absorbent paper or cloth, arrange in salad dish or bowl.

Grate carrot finely and fold into mayonnaise with mustard. If too thick, dilute with a little milk or cream. Spoon mayonnaise over cauliflower and dust with paprika pepper.

Rice salad

10 oz long grain rice (boiled and
  drained)
1 large red carrot (diced)
4 oz French beans (diced)
1 teacup peas
$\frac{1}{2}$ cucumber
2 caps of pimiento, or 2-3
  tomatoes
French dressing

This recipe serves 6 people.

Method
Cook the carrot, French beans,
and peas separately in boiling
salted water until just tender,
then drain and refresh them.
Skin and dice cucumber, shred
the pimientos (or skin and shred
tomatoes). Add all the vegetables to the rice and fork up
with enough French dressing to
moisten.

Rice and celery salad

8 oz long grain rice
1 head of celery (sliced)

For French dressing
2 tablespoons white wine
  vinegar
salt
pepper (ground from mill)
6 tablespoons salad oil
1 clove of garlic (bruised)
1 dessertspoon French (Dijon)
  mustard

Method
Cook the rice in plenty of boiling
salted water in a pan until tender.
Drain, refresh with a jug of cold
water and then drain again. Turn
on to a dish to dry. Slice the
celery and mix with the rice.

To prepare dressing : add
seasoning to vinegar, beat oil
in gradually ; when thick taste
for correct seasoning. Drop in a
bruised clove of garlic and leave
for about 10 minutes ; then
remove garlic and whisk in
French mustard. Fork this
dressing into the rice and celery.

Rice salad (with pistachio nuts)

10 oz long grain rice
3 oz pistachio nuts
¼ pint French dressing (see
  method)
¼ teaspoon ground cinnamon
salt and pepper
3 oz currants

Method
Cook the rice in plenty of boiling salted water for 10-12 minutes, drain and rinse with hot water. Leave rice to drain again, then turn it on to a large flat dish and allow to dry. Blanch, split and shred pistachio nuts.

Prepare the French dressing, using three parts of oil to one part of wine vinegar, and mixing the cinnamon with the salt and pepper.

Mix currants, rice and pistachio nuts together and moisten with the French dressing. Season with extra salt and pepper, if necessary.

Chestnut and celery salad

1 head of celery
¾ lb chestnuts
chicken, or turkey, stock — (see page 139)
1 tablespoon chopped parsley

For dressing
juice of 1 lemon
4 tablespoons oil
1 tablespoon caster sugar
salt and pepper
1-2 tablespoons cream (optional)

Method

Cut celery into 2-inch lengths and then down in sticks. Soak in ice-cold water for 1-2 hours.

Meanwhile peel and skin chestnuts. To do this, place them in a pan and cover with plenty of cold water. Bring to the boil and, once the water is bubbling well, remove pan from heat. Take out nuts with a draining spoon and hold with a cloth while stripping off peel and inner skin with a small sharp knife. (If skin doesn't come away easily, put nut back in water and bring to boil again, but don't leave nut in boiling water for more than ½ minute or it will cook and skin will be impossible to remove.) Simmer nuts in the stock until barely tender. Leave to cool in the stock and then drain.

Combine ingredients for the dressing in the order given. Drain and dry the celery thoroughly and put into a bowl with the chestnuts, mixing them both with the dressing. Turn the mixture into a salad bowl for serving and scatter the parsley over it.

Celery, potato and olive salad

½ lb new potatoes
1 head of celery (cut in short lengths)
2 oz black olives (halved and stoned)
1 dessert apple (diced)

For dressing
2 tablespoons tomato sauce, or ketchup
2-3 tablespoons double cream
1 tablespoon olive oil
lemon juice (to taste)
salt and pepper (to taste)
caster sugar (to taste)

Method

Boil the potatoes in their skins until just tender, remove skins, slice potatoes and put them into a bowl with the celery, the olives and the apple.

To prepare dressing: mix all the ingredients together. Spoon over the salad.

Serve with cold ham or tongue.

Celery and French bean salad

4 lb French beans (fresh, or frozen)
6 heads of celery, or 8, if very small
¾-1 pint French dressing

Method

If using fresh French beans, trim and cut them into lozenge-shapes before cooking; if using frozen beans, cook and cut them into lozenge-shapes after cooking. In both cases, cook beans until tender (about 10-15 minutes for fresh ones) in boiling, salted water, then drain and refresh them well, as this helps to preserve the colour.

Wash and trim the celery, cut into 1-inch pieces, then again into julienne strips. Leave these in ice-cold water until ready to use. Then drain and dry celery well, mix together with the French beans and add the French dressing. Turn into bowls for serving.

Lima bean salad

1 can (12 oz) Lima beans (drained)
4 tablespoons French dressing
3-4 sticks of celery
½ dill cucumber
1 tablespoon snipped chives

Method

Slice the celery and cucumber and mix with the Lima beans. Moisten with French dressing, add the chives and serve.

Serve with cold ham, tongue or salt beef.

Bean salad

4 oz dried brown beans, Italian or Dutch (soaked in water overnight)
bouquet of 1 bayleaf, 1 stick of celery and 4-5 parsley stalks
1 medium-size onion (finely sliced)
2 ripe, firm tomatoes
2 oz Dutch cheese (sliced and cut in shreds)
1 dessertspoon chopped parsley
salt
black pepper (ground from mill)
¼ pint lemon cream dressing

Method

Drain beans and put into a pan of fresh, slightly salted water. The beans must be brought to the boil very slowly, taking not less than 40 minutes. When they have boiled, add the bouquet, cover pan and simmer for 1 hour.

Cool slightly in the liquor, then drain. Simmer onion in a pan of salted water for 3-4 minutes) or until just tender, and drain. Scald and skin tomatoes, cut in half, remove seeds and hard core, and slice each piece into four. Put beans into a bowl with onion, tomatoes, cheese, parsley and seasoning to taste. Moisten well with the lemon cream dressing.

Bean, tomato and cucumber salad

¾ lb French beans
½-¾ lb tomatoes
1 cucumber
French dressing (made with 1 table-
    spoon wine vinegar, 3-4 table-
    spoons oil, salt and pepper ground
    from mill and squeeze of lemon
    juice — optional)

This is good served with cold
roast beef or roast chicken.

Method

Top and tail the beans and, if
necessary, run the peeler down
the sides of the beans to remove
any strings. Tie the beans in a
bundle and cook in plenty of
boiling salted water for about
20 minutes. When just tender,
lift out, dip into cold water to
refresh, then drain thoroughly.

Meanwhile scald, skin and
quarter the tomatoes and remove the seeds. Peel the
cucumber, quarter lengthways
and cut down into small chunks.
Mix ingredients for dressing.

Dress each of the vegetables
separately, then arrange them
on a dish with beans in the
centre and the tomatoes and
cucumber on either side.
Sprinkle with any remaining
dressing and serve chilled.

Rice and broad bean salad

8 oz thick grain rice
1 pint chicken stock (see page 139)
2 lb broad beans
¼–½ pint mayonnaise
salt and pepper
lemon juice (to taste)

Method
Wash rice well and cook until it is just tender and stock absorbed; leave until cold. Shell and cook beans, drain and remove their outside jackets. Mix beans and rice together, using a fork. Add enough mayonnaise to give a light creamy consistency. Season well and sharpen with a little lemon juice.

Serve with cold salt beef or cold lamb.

Cucumber salad 1

1 cucumber
salt
pepper (ground from mill)
caster sugar (to taste)
1 dessertspoon white wine vinegar

Method
Peel cucumber unless the skin is very tender, slice finely and sprinkle with salt; leave slices pressed between two plates in a cool place for 1 hour. Then tip off any liquid and add pepper, sugar and vinegar. Arrange slices in a serving dish.

Note : the following pages give some variations on the basic cucumber salad. Raita is particularly good with curries.

Cucumber salad 2

1 medium-size cucumber
salt
French dressing, or soured cream, or yoghourt
snipped chives

Method
Prepare cucumber as for Cucumber salad 1. After draining, pour over French dressing, or spoon over a little soured cream or yoghourt. Sprinkle with snipped chives.

Cucumber and bean salad

1 cucumber
½ lb French beans
French dressing

Method
Peel and split the cucumber in two. Scoop out the seeds and cut across into ½-inch slices. Blanch and refresh cucumber.

Trim beans and cut in 2-3 pieces ; boil them until just tender, drain and refresh.

Mix the beans and cucumber together in a salad bowl and moisten with French dressing.

Serve with escalope of veal or with cold salmon.

Cucumber and carrot salad

1 cucumber (finely sliced)
8 oz carrots (coarsely shredded)
2½ fl oz soured cream
salt
pepper (ground from mill)
caster sugar (to taste)
1-2 dessertspoons white wine
  vinegar

Method
Dégorge the cucumber. Mix the shredded carrots with the soured cream and season.

After 1 hour, drain the cucumber, season to taste with caster sugar, salt and pepper; then sprinkle over the wine vinegar. Pile the carrot mixture in the centre of a dish and surround with cucumber.

Cucumber and tomato salad

1 cucumber
1 lb tomatoes
salt
French dressing (made with
  3 tablespoons olive oil,
  1 tablespoon vinegar,
  seasoning and 1 tablespoon
  chopped parsley, mint and chives
  — mixed)

Method
Peel cucumber, cut into chunks, salt lightly, cover and leave in a cool place for 1 hour. Scald and skin tomatoes and cut each one into four, removing hard core and seeds. Tip off any liquid from the cucumber. Mix the prepared vegetables together and moisten with the dressing.

Sweet and sour cucumber

1 cucumber
salt
1 tablespoon caster sugar
1 tablespoon wine vinegar
black pepper (ground from mill)
lemon juice (to taste)
chopped mint (to garnish)

Method
Peel the cucumber, split it in half lengthways and then cut in slices; sprinkle with salt, cover with a plate and set in the refrigerator for 30 minutes. Meanwhile mix the sugar and vinegar together. On removing the cucumber from the refrigerator, drain off any liquid and add it to the sugar and vinegar; stir until the sugar has dissolved. Add black pepper and lemon juice to taste. Pour this liquid over the cucumber and garnish with mint before serving.

Raita

1 large cucumber
salt
1 carton (5 fl oz) plain
  yoghourt
black pepper
sugar (to taste)

Method
Peel the cucumber and grate coarsely on to a plate. Sprinkle with salt, cover and stand the plate in the refrigerator, or in a cold place, for 30 minutes. Then drain the cucumber thoroughly; mix it with the yoghourt in a bowl and add black pepper and sugar to taste.

Cucumber raita with chillies

1 cucumber
salt
2 chillies (seeds removed and
   flesh chopped)
1 carton (5 fl oz) plain
   yoghourt

Method
Peel the cucumber and shred on a coarse grater, sprinkle lightly with salt and leave for 1 hour.

Gently press off liquid from cucumber. Mix in the chillies and yoghourt and taste for more salt as needed. Chill and serve as an accompaniment to hot curries.

Florentine salad

8 oz thick grain rice
1 pint chicken stock (see page 139)
$\frac{1}{4}$ lb small flat black mushrooms
2 tablespoons olive oil
salt and pepper
$\frac{1}{4}$ pint mayonnaise
1 teaspoon chopped fennel, or
   dill

Method
Wash the rice until the water runs clear, then put it in a pan with the stock and cook until rice is tender and the stock absorbed; turn into a bowl to cool.

Wash and trim the mushrooms, then sauté them in the oil for 1 minute only; when cold, add them to the rice, season, and bind with the mayonnaise. Sprinkle with the herbs before serving.

Serve with cold roast veal.

Tomato salad with lemon dressing

$\frac{1}{2}$ lb tomatoes (ripe and firm)

For lemon dressing
1 tablespoon lemon juice
2 tablespoons oil
2 tablespoons single cream
$\frac{1}{2}$ teaspoon salt
1 rounded teaspoon caster sugar
pepper (ground from mill)
rind of $\frac{1}{2}$ lemon

Method
Scald, skin and slice tomatoes, then put them in a serving dish.

To prepare lemon dressing: beat all the ingredients (except rind) together and adjust seasoning. Cut lemon rind into fine shreds, blanch, drain and dry them; sprinkle over the dish.

Vichy salad

1 bunch of new carrots
$\frac{1}{4}$ pint mayonnaise
1 large teaspoon Dijon mustard
1 tablespoon double cream
1 tablespoon coarsely chopped
   parsley

Method
Scrape and quarter the carrots. Mix the mayonnaise with the mustard and cream, then stir it into the carrots. Turn them into an hors d'oeuvre dish and sprinkle well with parsley.

Serve with cold roast pork, cold beef, or cold chicken.

Courgette salad

1 lb small courgettes
2 shallots (finely chopped)
4 tablespoons olive oil
1 dessertspoon paprika pepper
salt and pepper
little caster sugar
1 teaspoon dill seeds, or a little
   fresh dill (chopped)
2 tablespoons wine vinegar

Method
Wipe the courgettes and slice thinly. Heat the oil in a deep frying, or sauté, pan (taking care not to get the oil too hot) then add the chopped shallots and the courgettes. Sauté slowly until the courgettes are partially cooked, then add the paprika seasoning, sugar, dill and vinegar. Continue to cook, turning frequently, for a further 5 minutes or until tender. Adjust seasoning and turn out to cool. Serve with cold roast beef or lamb, or as part of an hors d'oeuvre.

Les crudités

(Raw vegetable salad)

carrots
beetroot
swedes (preferably Cornish)
cabbage (drumhead, or Dutch)
celery
about ½ pint French dressing
1 bunch of watercress

This salad should be prepared 1 hour before serving.

Method
Grate the carrot, beetroot and swedes separately on a fine grater and put each vegetable into separate bowls. Finely shred the cabbage and celery separately and put into separate bowls. Moisten each vegetable with French dressing and carefully arrange each kind in sections in a large wooden or china salad bowl.

Set a bunch of watercress in the centre and serve the salad with hot rolls or a hot garlic loaf (see page 138). Hand a bowl of boiled dressing separately.

Basque salad

3 red peppers
$\frac{1}{2}$ lb tomatoes
1 teaspoon caster sugar
1 French roll
1 teaspoon tomato purée
1 teaspoon paprika pepper
$\frac{1}{2}$ teaspoon black pepper
1 clove of garlic (crushed with
$\frac{1}{4}$ teaspoon salt)
2 tablespoons red wine vinegar
6 tablespoons olive oil

Method

Roast the peppers under a red-hot grill until the skin is charred all over. Rinse them under the cold tap and scrape well; cut in half, scoop out the core and seeds, and shred flesh. Scald, skin and slice the tomatoes and dust very lightly with sugar.

Cut the French roll in $\frac{1}{2}$-inch slices and toast; when cold put slices at the bottom of a large gratin dish.

For the dressing; mix the tomato purée, paprika, pepper and garlic together with wine vinegar and whisk in oil.

Place the peppers and tomatoes on the toast and spoon over the dressing.

Serve with cold ham, cold fish such as soused mackerel, or cold roast beef.

Basque salad is served on small rounds of toast as an accompaniment to cold meat or fish

Catherine-wheel salad

Foundation dough
8 oz plain flour
½ teaspoon salt
½ oz yeast
1 teaspoon sugar
2½ fl oz milk (warmed)
2 eggs (beaten)
2 oz butter (creamed)
extra butter and little French
    mustard, or cream cheese
    (flavoured to taste)

For topping
beetroot (coarsely grated)
French dressing
cucumber (thinly sliced)
carrot (grated)
tomatoes (skinned, thinly sliced)
onion (cut into rings and
    blanched)
coleslaw (see page 118)

Method
Sift the flour and salt in a warmed mixing bowl. Cream the yeast and sugar and add this to the warmed milk with the beaten eggs. Then add all the liquid to the flour and beat thoroughly. Work the creamed butter into the paste. Cover and leave for 40 minutes to rise.

Set the oven at 400°F or Mark 6. Pat out the dough on to a floured baking sheet in as large a round as possible. Allow to prove for 15 minutes, then bake in pre-set oven for about 30 minutes.

When cold, split the round in two and sandwich with the extra butter, flavoured with French mustard, or with the flavoured creamed cheese.

Start arranging the salads in the centre and work out towards the edge, beginning with the beetroot, mixed with a little French dressing. Surround this with the cucumber, then grated carrot. Then arrange the tomato slices, overlapping them, and between each slice place a thinly cut onion ring. Round the tomatoes, arrange the coleslaw. Continue in this way until the whole surface is covered.

Russian salad

1 large carrot (diced)
3 oz peas
$\frac{1}{2}$ lb potatoes (boiled and diced)
$\frac{1}{4}$ pint mayonnaise (made with 1 egg yolk, $\frac{1}{4}$ pint oil, salt, pepper, pinch of dry mustard)

Method
Cook diced carrot and peas and allow to cool. Combine all the vegetables, using the mayonnaise (previously thinned with a little boiling water) to bind them together.

Spanish salad

$\frac{3}{4}$ lb tomatoes
1 large Spanish onion
1 green pepper
salt and pepper
French dressing (made with 2 tablespoons white wine and 6 tablespoons olive oil)
1 tablespoon mixed chopped herbs (parsley, lemon thyme)

Method
Scald, skin and slice the tomatoes. Cut the onion and pepper in rings, removing the latter's centre core and seeds.

Put the onion into pan of cold water, bring to the boil, then add the green pepper and boil for 1 minute; drain and refresh.

Mix the tomatoes, onion and pepper together in a salad bowl, season, spoon over the French dressing and dust with herbs.

Serve with cold roast chicken.

Mixed vegetable salad

1 hard white Dutch cabbage (weighing 3 lb)
1 lb carrots
1 head of celery
6 tablespoons olive oil
salt
pepper (ground from mill)
4 crisp dessert apples
3 tablespoons white wine vinegar
2$\frac{1}{2}$ fl oz soured, or fresh, cream

Method
Shred cabbage very finely and soak in ice-cold water while preparing the other ingredients.

Peel and grate carrots. Wash celery and cut in julienne strips.

Drain cabbage and place it in a large bowl; add oil and mix thoroughly until every shred is well coated, then add seasoning to taste.

Peel, core and slice the apples and mix with the cabbage. Add the carrot and celery and wine vinegar and cream and mix until thoroughly blended. Adjust the seasoning and serve salad in large bowls.

Cutting celery into julienne strips for mixed vegetable salad

Coleslaw salad

1 small hard white, or Dutch, cabbage
$\frac{1}{4}$ pint boiled dressing, or less of French dressing
salt and pepper
1 dessert apple, Cox's or Jonathan
grated carrot (optional)
paprika pepper, or parsley (chopped)

Method
Cut cabbage into four, trim away hard stalk, then slice into thin strips. Put in a mixing bowl, add the boiled or French dressing and extra seasoning to taste. Thoroughly coat every piece of cabbage, then add apple (cored and sliced but not peeled), and grated carrot. Mix well, cover and leave for 2-3 hours before serving. Pile in a dish and sprinkle with paprika or parsley.

Coleslaw, although originally an American dish, owes its name to the Dutch from the time they took over Manhattan Island. In Dutch, kool (cabbage) and sla (salad).

Turnip salad

1 lb small turnips
1 large Spanish onion
2 tablespoons white wine vinegar
salt and pepper
1 tablespoon soft brown sugar
3 tablespoons olive oil
1 tablespoon grated horseradish
1 tablespoon double cream

This dish should be served as an accompaniment to cold roast beef.

Method
Peel and grate the turnips. Chop the onion very finely and then mix with turnip in a bowl. Mix seasoning, sugar and vinegar together, whisk in the oil and add the horseradish mixed with the cream. Pour this mixture over the vegetables, stir well, cover the bowl and chill salad for 24 hours before serving.

Salade niçoise

2 lb tomatoes
2 lb French beans
1 cucumber (peeled and shredded)
$\frac{1}{4}$ lb black olives (stoned)
$\frac{1}{4}$ pint French dressing

Method
Scald, skin and quarter tomatoes. Cut beans into large diamonds and boil until tender; drain and refresh. Mix all the ingredients together and moisten with French dressing.

Salad composé

4 oz rice
½ lb tomatoes
4 oz small white button
  mushrooms
1 tablespoon olive oil
3 oz black olives
French dressing (made with white
  wine in place of vinegar)

*Tomatoes, mushrooms, black olives
and rice make up salad composé*

Method
Boil and drain the rice. Scald
and skin tomatoes, quarter them
and remove seeds; halve each
quarter.
  Leave mushrooms whole and
sauté them in oil. Halve and
stone the olives. Combine all
the ingredients in a salad bowl
and moisten with French
dressing.
  Serve with grilled steak or
pork chops.

Vegetable salad

1 Spanish onion (finely sliced and
  separated into rings)
2 cucumbers (peeled and sliced)
1 head of celery (washed and
  sliced)
salsa verde (see page 133)
1 bunch of radishes

Method
Blanch the onion, then drain,
put into fresh cold water, bring
once more to the boil and cook
for 7-8 minutes, drain and
refresh. The onion should be
lightly crisp but not too soft.
Put the cucumber slices into
iced water for 15 minutes, then
drain and dry well with absorbent paper or cloth. Arrange the
cucumbers, onion and celery in
layers, piling them up into a
pyramid. Pour salsa verde over
the vegetables and garnish with
the radishes, sliced or in roses.

Swiss salad

1½ lb leaf spinach
vinegar and olive oil (to
  moisten)
salt and pepper
6 oz Gruyère cheese
chives (to finish)

For dressing
juice of 1 lemon
salt and pepper
caster sugar (to taste)
4 tablespoons oil
¼ pint double cream

To serve cold for a lunch dish
with a hot garlic loaf (see page
138).

Method
Blanch the spinach in plenty
of water for 5-6 minutes then
drain and press well to remove
all liquid. Mix it with a little
vinegar and oil and season.
Turn into a dish to serve. Slice
the cheese and arrange on top.
  Mix the ingredients for the
dressing in the order given and
then spoon it over the cheese.
Snip some chives on top.

Avocado pear salad

2 avocado pears
1 Iceberg, or Webb's, lettuce

For dressing
juice of $\frac{1}{2}$ lemon
1 teaspoon caster sugar
$\frac{1}{2}$ teaspoon salt
$\frac{1}{4}$ teaspoon black pepper (ground
    from mill)
6 tablespoons salad oil

Method
Wash and dry the lettuce very well and pull into small pieces. Peel the avocado pears and cut in thin slices, discarding the stone. Whisk all ingredients for the dressing together and spoon over the lettuce and avocado pieces in a bowl. Turn over carefully as the avocado will break and spoil the appearance of the finished salad unless handled with great care.

Artichoke and tomato salad

1$\frac{1}{2}$ lb jerusalem artichokes
salted water
squeeze of lemon juice
4-5 tomatoes (according to size)

For dressing
1 carton (5 fl oz) plain yoghourt
2-3 tablespoons double cream
salt and pepper
1 teaspoon caster sugar
squeeze of lemon juice
1 dessertspoon snipped chives, or
    chopped parsley

Method
Peel artichokes and cut into walnut-size pieces. Cook in pan of salted water with a good squeeze of lemon juice until just tender (about 7-8 minutes). Drain, rinse in cold water and drain again. Put in a bowl with tomatoes (skinned, seeds removed, flesh shredded).

To prepare dressing: turn yoghourt into a bowl, whip the cream lightly, add to yoghourt with the seasoning, sugar and lemon juice. Add chives or parsley. Mix together with artichokes and tomatoes.

Beetroot relish

2 large cooked beetroots
2 tart dessert, or cooking, apples
3-4 tablespoons French dressing
   (with a little garlic added)

Method
Grate the beetroots coarsely;
peel, quarter and core the
apples and cut into dice. Mix
with the beetroot and moisten
with a little of the French
dressing. Pile into a dish for
serving.

Onion relish

2 Spanish onions
4-6 oz mushrooms
squeeze of lemon juice
salt and pepper
French dressing
1 dessertspoon chopped parsley
   (optional)

Method
Cut the onion into slices and
push out into rings. Put the
rings into cold water, bring
to the boil, drain and then
repeat this process and simmer
until barely cooked. Drain
thoroughly.

   Meanwhile slice the mushrooms thickly and barely cook
with a little water and the
lemon juice; season. Drain and
mix with the onion. Moisten
with a little French dressing and
the chopped parsley, if liked.
Pile into a dish for serving.

Tomato and anchovy relish

about $\frac{3}{4}$ lb tomatoes
about 1 dessertspoon anchovy
   essence
1 tablespoon vinegar
3 tablespoons oil
1 tablespoon double cream
pepper (ground from mill)

Method
Skin and quarter tomatoes;
remove seeds. Combine all the
liquid ingredients to make a
dressing and season well with
pepper. Add dressing to
tomatoes and pile into a dish
for serving.

Celery and cheese relish

1 head of celery
1-2 green peppers
4-6 oz mild Cheddar, or Gouda,
   cheese (diced)
French, or cream, dressing

Method
Clean the celery and chop
coarsely. Chop and blanch the
peppers, drain and mix with
the celery. Add the cheese and
moisten with French (or cream)
dressing. Pile into a dish for
serving.

Note : although called 'relishes'
these salads do not keep like
pickle and some chutneys.

Pickles, chutneys and vinegars

In the late summer, the cook has her last opportunity to stock up the family store cupboard in preparation for the year ahead. Now is the time to put up sweet and sour vegetable and fruit pickles, chutneys and bottled sauces. From such a well stocked store cupboard can come the perfect accompaniment for almost every dish from bread and butter to curries, cold meats or game.

These are not strictly salads, but we have included them in this book for those times when you would like a salad but, perhaps because of a change in family plans, you have no fresh greens to hand. The vinegars at the end of this section will help you bring a different flavour to your salad dressings.

It is important when pickling or spicing vegetables and fruit that they be of top quality. You should use an expensive, top-quality vinegar as well. For pickling, most vegetables are first washed and then salted, or soaked in brine. For preference use block salt instead of packet salt, grinding it down to a powder (rub the block on a grater or cut it in halves and rub the halves together) before using. After salting, the vegetables are rinsed, then packed into jars and covered with spiced vinegar. White malt distilled, or good wine, vinegar is the best to use. The most important point is that the vinegar be of good quality so as to contain the amount of acetic acid necessary for the vegetables to be preserved.

Sharp lemon pickle

7 medium-size juicy lemons
  (with thin skins)
1½ tablespoons salt
1 lb seedless raisins
1 teaspoon chilli powder
1 tablespoon pounded fresh
  ginger
4 cloves of garlic (crushed with
  salt)
½ pint mild vinegar
1¼ lb soft brown sugar
2 teaspoons grated horseradish

4-5 one lb screw-top glass jars

This pickle keeps well. Washed, but unpeeled, limes can be used in place of lemons.

Method
Cut lemons in eighths, remove the pips and hard ends, put in a large basin, sprinkle with salt, cover and leave them for 48 hours, stirring occasionally.

Drain the lemons and reserve the liquid. Mince the raisins, lemons and add the chilli powder, ginger and garlic. Put into an enamel pan, add the reserved liquid and vinegar; stir in the sugar and horseradish. Simmer until thick, stirring to prevent sticking. When quite cold put it into glass jars and screw them down tightly.

Mango chutney 1

6 mangoes (barely ripe)
2 tablespoons syrup (from
  preserved ginger)
4 oz seedless raisins
2 oz preserved ginger (chopped)
½ teaspoon chilli powder
½ teaspoon cumin seeds
1 tablespoon salt
2 cloves of garlic (crushed with
  salt)
3 tablespoons lemon juice
¾ pint white wine vinegar
1 lb granulated sugar

4-5 one lb screw-top glass jars

This kind of mango chutney is suitable for bottling.

Method
Peel the mangoes over a bowl and cut the pulp from the stones in slices. Put slices into an enamel pan with any juice and the syrup, add the raisins, chopped ginger, spices, salt, garlic and lemon juice. Pour over the vinegar, add sugar, and simmer gently in an uncovered pan until the liquid has thickened and the mango slices look syrupy. Pour into glass jars and screw down tightly.

Mango chutney 2

1 ripe mango
1 chilli (seeds removed and
    flesh finely chopped)
1 teaspoon grated fresh ginger
1½ teaspoons grated onion
1 dessertspoon vinegar
pinch of salt
pinch of granulated sugar

Method

Peel the mango and crush it finely with a fork, then add the chilli, ginger and onion. Put in a small bowl and sprinkle over 1 dessertspoon vinegar and a pinch each of salt and sugar. This chutney cannot be bottled, so serve it immediately.

Pimiento, apple and raisin chutney

1 cap of pimiento, or green
    pepper (coarsely chopped)
1 apple (peeled, cored and
    chopped)
1 tablespoon seedless raisins
    (halved if large)
pinch of cayenne pepper
pinch of paprika pepper
¼ teaspoon salt
pinch of granulated sugar
juice of a lemon

Method

Mix all the ingredients together, add the salt and a pinch of sugar to taste, and lemon juice to sharpen. This chutney cannot be bottled, so serve it immediately.

Gooseberry pickle

1 quart unripe gooseberries
½ lb demerara sugar
salt
1 quart white wine vinegar
½ lb mustard seeds
6 oz garlic
¾ lb stoned raisins
½ oz cayenne pepper

Method

Place the gooseberries in a pan with the sugar and salt and 1 pint of the vinegar. Stir over gentle heat until the sugar dissolves, then bring to the boil and cook until the gooseberries are tender. Bruise the mustard seeds, chop and crush the garlic and mix both with the raisins and cayenne. Put in a bowl and pour the boiling gooseberries over this, adding the remaining pint of cold vinegar. Pour into Kilner jars, screw down and store for at least six months before using.

Spiced rhubarb

rhubarb
$\frac{1}{2}$ lb granulated sugar to every
  2 lb fruit
1 quart white distilled vinegar
  to every 2 lb fruit
1 tablespoon mixed pickling
  spice
$\frac{1}{2}$-inch piece of stick cinnamon

Method
Wipe the rhubarb, cut it into pieces about $1\frac{1}{2}$ inches long and place in a mixing bowl with the sugar. Boil the spices with the vinegar and pour over the fruit and sugar. Leave for 24 hours.

Strain off the liquid, boil it for 5 minutes, pour it over the fruit and leave to stand for 10 minutes. Heat the fruit and liquid together carefully, without letting fruit boil. Turn into a mixing bowl and, when it is quite cold, put into small pots and tie them down securely, as for jam.

Spiced pineapple

1 large can pineapple slices
$2\frac{1}{2}$ fl oz white wine
2 tablespoons granulated sugar
$\frac{1}{2}$-inch stick of cinnamon
6 peppercorns
1 clove
2 tablespoons wine vinegar

Method
Strain pineapple slices and set aside; place syrup from pineapple in a pan with wine and sugar and dissolve over gentle heat. Add spices and boil for 5 minutes. Add the vinegar to the pan and boil rapidly until well reduced and thick; strain liquid over the pineapple slices and chill before serving.

This cannot be stored.

Spiced oranges

10 large sweet oranges
1 pint white wine vinegar
$2\frac{1}{2}$ lb lump sugar
4-inch stick of cinnamon
14 cloves
6 blades of mace

Serves 12 people.

These go well with cold meat. Use 2 lb screw-top jars.

Method
Cut the oranges into slices $\frac{1}{4}$ inch thick and put them in a pan with water just to cover. Put the lid half on the pan and simmer the slices until the peel is tender (about 1 hour).

Put the vinegar, sugar and spices into a preserving pan and boil for 5 minutes.

Drain the orange slices but reserve the liquor. Put about half the orange slices in the syrup and simmer gently for about 30 minutes.

Watchpoint It is most important that the orange slices are fully covered by the syrup, so it is advisable to cook them in two batches.

Lift out the cooked slices with a draining spoon into a bowl. Add the rest of the oranges to the pan and, if not covered by the remaining syrup, add a little of the reserved orange liquor. Cook as before. Turn into a bowl, cover with a plate and leave overnight.

The next morning tip off any remaining syrup and boil it until thick. Add the oranges and reboil. If the syrup is already thick, merely heat it slowly to boiling point, with the orange slices. Fill into warm dry preserving jars and cover at once.

Rose petal vinegar

1 pint dark red rose petals
  (preferably from damask
  roses)
1 pint white distilled vinegar
2 oz caster sugar

This looks pretty and gives a flavour of roses to a salad, especially if the dark red, old-fashioned damask rose is used. The petals should be pressed down into the measure.

Method
Wipe the rose petals carefully and place in a large jar. Dissolve the sugar in the vinegar over gentle heat. When cold, pour over the rose petals. Leave, covered, for 3-4 weeks, then strain off and bottle.

Cucumber vinegar

8 small ridge cucumbers
2-3 pints white wine, or white
  distilled, vinegar
2 medium-size onions (chopped)
1 rounded dessertspoon salt
good dash of Tabasco sauce, or
  pinch of cayenne pepper
fresh dill (optional)

Method
Peel and coarsely chop the cucumbers and place in a pan with the onion, salt, Tabasco (or cayenne) and pour on enough vinegar just to cover. Boil for 3 minutes, then pour off and leave, covered, for 6-7 days. Strain off the vinegar, bottle and cork well. If wished, a piece of fresh dill may be put into each bottle. Use for fish dressings and cucumber salads.

Horseradish preserve/vinegar

horseradish roots
white, or spiced, distilled vinegar
salt
caster sugar
fresh chillies

If you have horseradish roots in your garden, or can buy them locally, this is a good preserve to make at home as it has more flavour than the bought variety and is also cheaper.

Method
Wash and peel the horseradish roots; then grate immediately. Put into small jars about two-thirds full. Add 1 teaspoon salt, $\frac{1}{2}$ teaspoon sugar, and a small piece of fresh chilli to each jar. Fill to the top with white, or spiced, vinegar. Cover well with paper or screw down the lid.
Watchpoint If a metal lid is used, it must be lined with greaseproof paper.

To use, strain off the vinegar and press the horseradish lightly to remove any surplus liquid. It is then ready to use in a sauce, or it may be sprinkled over beetroot salad. The vinegar can be used for salad dressings.

Summer vinegar

nasturtium flowers
white wine vinegar
good pinch of salt
$\frac{1}{2}$ teaspoon cayenne pepper

Method

Pick the flowers on a dry day and fill a large Kilner jar, pressing down well. Add a good pinch of salt and the cayenne pepper, cover with vinegar and seal the jar tightly. After 2 days, fill the jar with extra vinegar and leave for at least 10 days. Then strain and bottle.

This vinegar is good with fish.

Chilli vinegar

about 50 red, or green, chillies
2 pints white distilled vinegar

This is better made with red chillies as they are riper and therefore hotter.

Method

Split the chillies in half. Boil the vinegar, add the chillies and bring back to the boil. Turn into a jar and leave, covered, for 5-6 weeks. If using green chillies, leave a further week as the flavour is less strong.

Strain off the vinegar and bottle it.

Note : use only a drop or two for a spicy salad; do not use in an oil and vinegar dressing.

Some of the ingredients for making home-made vinegars

129

Herb vinegars

These are simple and inexpensive to make at home; the leaves are infused or steeped in vinegar for a certain period of time. Once made, strain the vinegar off and bottle and label it. Apart from your own consumption, these make nice presents to give to friends and relations.

Herb vinegars should be made just before the plants flower. Use large jars (the 7 lb stone gallipot is good but must be tied down with foil). Glass screw-top jars of 1 lb and over are also suitable, but keep these in the dark while steeping the herbs. These vinegars can be used for flavouring salads, dressings and sauces.

Tarragon vinegar

4-6 oz tarragon to 2 pints white wine vinegar

Method
Use leaves and tender part of the stalks. Bruise them, pack into a jar to fill it well. Then fill jar with cold white wine vinegar, screw or tie down and leave for 6-8 weeks. Strain off and bottle. Put 2-3 sprigs of tarragon in each bottle before pouring in the strained vinegar. Cork or screw tightly.

Mint vinegar

4-6 oz mint to 2 pints white, or red, wine vinegar

Method
Use the Bowles variety of mint for preference.

Strip the leaves from stalks, then wash and dry them well. Pack leaves into jars, barely cover with cold wine vinegar. Cover and leave it for 3-4 weeks before straining and bottling.

Use for salad dressing (French, vinaigrette etc.) and mint sauce.

Celery vinegar

1 large head of celery
2 pints white wine vinegar
1 tablespoon celery seeds
1 tablespoon salt
1 tablespoon caster sugar

Method
Slice the celery thinly and place in a large jar with the celery seeds. Place the vinegar, salt and sugar in a pan and bring to the boil; pour this over the celery. Leave, covered, for 2-3 weeks, then strain and bottle. Use in summer salads and dressings.

Salad dressings

Though the first requirement of any salad is that it should be fresh and young, the second is that the dressing should be good. A good salad dressing is piquant but not strong, it will never mask the flavour either of salad vegetables or any dish accompanying the salad. It will in fact refresh the palate, enhance the flavour of the vegetables and complement the main dish. These facts apply whether we are talking about the classic French dressing, a mayonnaise, or any of the numerous variations possible. One point that is worth mentioning in passing is that a tart, vinegary salad dressing will ruin any wine you may have chosen to drink with your meal — so if you are drinking wine be particularly careful.

Probably the most popular salad dressing the world over is the simplest, the French dressing. Properly made, with a good wine vinegar and a first class oil, this dressing will grace any meal. English people will often experiment with this and conclude that it is too oily for their tastes; this is usually either because they have not used enough salt, or because they have used malt vinegar. A much pleasanter result is produced with a red or white wine vinegar (the red is milder than the white). The quality of the oil is also important as poor oils have a particularly unpleasant flavour. Use either the finest olive oil you can get or one of the tasteless, vegetable oils now on the market.

A rich mayonnaise, made from egg yolks, oil and vinegar, adds nourishment to any salad, and is the right one to choose for many of the more substantial ones. Do allow yourself time to make it properly, though; if the oil is added faster than a drop or two at a time, the dressing will curdle.

To save time, have French dressing and a thick mayonnaise ready made and stored, covered, in a jar or container. This can be kept for a week or two in a cool larder, or refrigerator. If you keep mayonnaise in a refrigerator, be sure to take it out at least 2 hours before use and leave it at room temperature; should it curdle or separate, add 1 tablespoon of boiling water and whisk well.

There are many other salad dressings, of course. Some variations may be produced simply by using the flavoured vinegars on pages 128 to 130 instead of a plain wine one. Others are to be found in this section. You will find guidance on using them among the recipes for salads in other sections of the book.

French dressing

1 tablespoon vinegar (red or
  white wine, cider, or tarragon)
3 tablespoons olive oil, or
  groundnut oil
$\frac{1}{2}$ teaspoon salt
$\frac{1}{2}$ teaspoon black pepper
  (ground from mill)
good pinch of sugar (optional)

Method
Mix the vinegar with the
seasonings, add the oil and
when the dressing thickens,
taste for correct seasoning. More
salt should be added if the
dressing is sharp yet oily.
Quantities should be in the ratio
of 1 part vinegar to 3 parts oil.

Vinaigrette dressing

Add fresh chopped herbs, eg,
thyme, marjoram, basil or
parsley, to the French dressing
recipe given above.

Mayonnaise

2 egg yolks
salt and pepper
dry mustard
$\frac{3}{4}$ cup of salad oil
2 tablespoons wine vinegar

This recipe makes $\frac{1}{2}$ pint. Eggs
should not come straight from
the refrigerator. If oil is cloudy
or chilled, warm it by putting
bottle in a pan of hot water for
a short time.

Method
Work egg yolks and seasonings
with a small whisk or wooden
spoon in a bowl until thick;
then start adding the oil drop
by drop. This must be done very
carefully to prevent mayonnaise
curdling. When 2 tablespoons
of oil have been added this
mixture will be very thick. Now
carefully stir in 1 teaspoon of
the vinegar.

The remaining oil can then be
added a little more quickly,
either 1 tablespoon at a time
and beaten thoroughly between
each addition until it is absorbed, or in a thin steady
stream if you are using an
electric beater. When all the oil
has been absorbed, add remaining vinegar to taste, and
extra salt and pepper as necessary.

To thin and lighten mayonnaise add a little hot water. For
a coating consistency, thin with
a little cream or milk.

Note : if mayonnaise curdles,
start with a fresh yolk in another
bowl and work well with
seasoning, then add the curdled
mixture to it very slowly and
carefully. When curdled mixture
is completely incorporated, more
oil can be added if the mixture
is too thin.

Boiled dressing

1 tablespoon caster sugar
1 dessertspoon plain flour
1 teaspoon salt
1 dessertspoon made mustard
1 tablespoon water
$\frac{1}{4}$ pint each vinegar and water
  (mixed)
1 egg
$\frac{1}{2}$ oz butter
cream, or creamy milk

Method
Mix dry ingredients together,
add mustard and about 1 tablespoon of water. Add to vinegar
and water and cook thoroughly
for about 5 minutes. Beat egg,
add butter, pour on the hot
vinegar mixture and beat
thoroughly.

When cold dilute with cream
or milk and mix well. This
dressing keeps well, covered, in
a refrigerator.

Lemon cream dressing

$\frac{1}{4}$ pint mayonnaise
$\frac{1}{4}$ pint cream (lightly whipped)
grated rind and juice of $\frac{1}{2}$ lemon
salt and pepper
made mustard

Method
Stir the cream into the mayonnaise, adding the grated rind
and lemon juice gradually.
Season well; add mustard to
taste. Add 1 tablespoon of
boiling water, if necessary, as
the dressing should be thin. (It
can be made with less cream
and more mayonnaise.)

Mayonnaise Nantua

3 oz shrimps, or prawns (with
  shells)
$\frac{1}{2}$ pint olive oil
2-3 egg yolks
$\frac{1}{2}$ teaspoon paprika pepper
salt and pepper
about 1$\frac{1}{2}$-2 dessertspoons white
  wine vinegar (to taste)

Method
Shell the shrimps (or the prawns).
Pound the shells with the paprika in the oil and leave to
soak for 10-15 minutes. Chop
prawns roughly, or leave shrimps
whole, and strain the oil.

Prepare the mayonnaise (see
method, page 132). When all the
oil has been absorbed, add
remaining vinegar to taste, extra
seasoning, if necessary, and
the shrimps (or prawns).

Note : serve with a cold fish
such as salmon or sea tront.

Salsa verde

1 large handful of parsley
1 rounded tablespoon capers
1-2 cloves of garlic
1-2 anchovy fillets
3-5 tablespoons olive oil
1 slice of white bread (crust
  removed)
1 tablespoon lemon juice
salt and pepper

Method
Pick the parsley from the stalks,
chop it; pound or blend with
capers, garlic and anchovies.
Spoon 1-2 tablespoons of oil
over the bread and, when
soaked, add to the parsley
mixture and continue to pound.
Gradually add 2-3 tablespoons
of oil; add lemon juice and
season well. The sauce should
be thick.

Roquefort dressing

2 oz Roquefort cheese
1 teaspoon Worcestershire sauce
2 tablespoons double cream
4-5 tablespoons French dressing
$\frac{1}{2}$ teaspoon finely grated onion

Method

First prepare the dressing. Work the Roquefort until quite smooth, adding the Worcestershire sauce and cream, then gradually the French dressing and finely grated onion.

Scandinavian dressing

1 dessertspoon caraway, or dill seeds (crushed)
$\frac{1}{4}$ pint water (boiling)
1 teaspoon salt
$1\frac{1}{2}$ tablespoons vinegar
2 teaspoons caster sugar

Method

Make caraway liquid by crushing 1 dessertspoon caraway seeds (or dill) and scald with $\frac{1}{4}$ pint boiling water. Cool and strain. Reserve $2\frac{1}{2}$ tablespoons of caraway liquid and store remaining liquid in a screw-top jar for future use. It will keep up to 2 weeks in a cool place.

Add other ingredients to caraway liquid and mix all together. This dressing is good with a plain beetroot side salad.

Tarragon cream dressing

1 egg
2 rounded tablespoons caster sugar
3 tablespoons tarragon vinegar
salt and pepper
$\frac{1}{4}$ pint double cream

Method

Break egg into a bowl and beat with a fork. Add caster sugar and then gradually add the tarragon vinegar. Stand the bowl in a pan of boiling water and stir mixture until it begins to thicken. Draw off heat and continue stirring. When mixture has consistency of thick cream take the basin out of the pan and stir for a few seconds longer. Season lightly and leave until cold.

Meanwhile, partially whip the double cream; fold this into the cold dressing and season to taste.

This dressing can be made in large quantities (omitting the cream) and kept in a screw-top jar in the refrigerator for up to 3 weeks. The cream is then added just before using.

Soured cream dressing

1 clove garlic (crushed with a little salt)
1 large carton (7 fl oz) soured, or cultured, cream
pepper (ground from the mill)
lemon juice, or wine vinegar to taste
1 teaspoon paprika pepper (optional)

Method

Work the crushed garlic and, if wished, the paprika into the cream. Season with pepper and add lemon juice, or wine vinegar, to taste.

Appendix

Notes and basic recipes

Almonds

Buy them with their skins on. This way they retain their oil better. Blanching to remove the skins gives extra juiciness.

To blanch : pour boiling water over the shelled nuts, cover the pan and leave until cool. Then the skins can be easily removed (test one with finger and thumb). Drain, rinse in cold water, press skins off with fingers. Rinse, dry thoroughly.

To brown almonds : blanch and bake for 7-8 minutes in a moderate oven at 350°F or Mark 4.

To chop almonds : first blanch, skin, chop and then brown them in the oven, if desired.

To shred almonds : first blanch, skin, split in two and cut each half lengthways in fine pieces. These can then be used as they are or browned quickly in the oven, with or without a sprinkling of caster sugar.

To flake almonds : first blanch, skin, and cut horizontally into flakes with a small sharp knife.

To grind almonds : first blanch, skin, chop and pound into a paste (use a pestle and mortar, or a grinder, or the butt end of a rolling pin). Home-prepared ground almonds taste much better than the ready-ground variety.

Asparagus (or sprue, the slender variety)

To prepare : trim the bottom stalks of the asparagus, leaving about 2-3 inches before the green starts. To make sure that all stalks are the same length, cut them while asparagus is still tied in bundles. After untying them, rinse stalks well in cold water and then, using a small vegetable knife, scrape the white part of the stems well and stand them in a bowl of cold water. Now tie the spears together in bundles, according to size, with fine string ; leave the cut stems standing in cold water until you are ready to cook them.

Have ready a deep pan of plenty of boiling salted water and stand the asparagus spears in this, stalk end down ; cook gently, covered, for 12-15 minutes or until the green part is tender.

Watchpoint The green tips should stand above the water and cook just in the steam.

Aspic jelly

This is a jelly made from good fish, chicken, or meat stock very slightly sharpened with wine and a few drops of wine vinegar. Care must be taken that the stock is well flavoured and seasoned and that it is not too sharp, only pleasantly acidulated.

With certain delicately flavoured foods, such as fish, eggs or prawns, home-made aspic adds to and enhances the flavour. If you need aspic for brushing over sliced meat, use the commercially prepared variety, which is excellent for this — especially if a small quantity of the water is replaced by sherry. Make up according to directions on the packet or can.

Aspic, and most jellies containing wine, will keep for several days in the refrigerator. To do this, pour the liquid aspic into a jug, leave to set, then pour about $\frac{1}{2}$ inch cold water over the top, and refrigerate. Remember to pour water off before melting the aspic for use.

Basic aspic recipe

$2\frac{1}{2}$ fl oz sherry
$2\frac{1}{2}$ fl oz white wine
2 oz gelatine
$1\frac{3}{4}$ pints cold stock
1 teaspoon wine vinegar
2 egg whites

Method

Add wines to gelatine and set

aside. Pour cold stock into scalded pan, add vinegar. Whisk egg whites to a froth, add them to the pan, set over moderate heat and whisk backwards and downwards (the reverse of the usual whisking movement) until the stock is hot. Then add gelatine, which by now will have absorbed the wine, and continue whisking steadily until boiling point is reached.

Stop whisking and allow liquid to rise to the top of the pan; turn off heat or draw pan aside and leave to settle for about 5 minutes, then bring it again to the boil, draw pan aside once more and leave liquid to settle. At this point the liquid should look clear; if not, repeat the boiling-up process.

Filter the jelly through a scalded cloth or jelly bag.

The aspic should be allowed to cool before use.

The stock for aspic jelly may be white (chicken or veal), brown (beef) or fish, according to the dish being made.

Baked (jacket) potatoes

1 large potato per person
salt
pat of butter per person
parsley (optional)

Method

Well scrub large, even-size potatoes and roll them in salt. Bake for 1½ hours (or until they give when pressed) in an oven at 375°F or Mark 4. Make crosscuts on top of each potato and squeeze to enlarge cuts. Put a pat of butter and sprig of parsley in centre; serve at once.

Béchamel sauce

¾ pint milk
slice of onion
6 peppercorns

1 blade of mace
1 bayleaf
1 tablespoon cream (optional)

For roux
1 oz butter
2 tablespoons flour
salt and pepper

Method

Infuse milk with onion and spices in a covered pan over a low heat for 5-7 minutes, but do not boil. Pour the milk into a basin and wipe the pan out.

To make the roux: melt the butter slowly, remove pan from heat and stir in the flour. Pour on at least one-third of the milk through a strainer and blend together with a wooden spoon. Then add the rest of the milk, season lightly, return to heat and stir until boiling. Boil for not more than 2 minutes, then taste for seasoning. The sauce may be finished with 1 tablespoon of cream.

Butter beans (dried)

Preparation and cooking:

1 Wash the beans and pick them over to remove any grit or small stones.

2 Soak them in plenty of tepid water for 8 hours, or leave overnight. If they have to be left longer, change the water or they may start to ferment.

3 Drain them, cover with plenty of fresh warm water and cook in a covered pan. If the water is hard, add a pinch of bicarbonate of soda which will help to soften the outer skins. Salt is never added at this stage as it would harden them. Bring them very slowly to boiling point, allowing 30-40 minutes, then simmer gently for about 1 hour. Drain them again and then use as specified in the recipe.

Court bouillon (for shellfish)

2 medium-size onions (sliced)
1 carrot (sliced)
$\frac{1}{2}$ oz butter
juice of $\frac{1}{2}$ lemon
bouquet garni
6 peppercorns
2 pints water
$\frac{1}{4}$ pint white wine
1 teaspoon salt

Method
Soften the onions and carrot slowly in the butter, using a pan large enough to hold the shellfish. Add remaining ingredients and simmer together for 15-20 minutes.

Curd cheese

Curd cheese cannot be made with pasteurised milk, as the bacteria which cause the natural souring of the milk are destroyed in the pasteurisation process. Non-pasteurised milk is obtainable in the country and in certain other areas. Alternatively, curd cheese can be bought in delicatessens or large supermarkets.

In warm weather (or at a warm temperature) milk sours more quickly. This is desirable, as the quicker it sours the less likely it is that the resulting curd or cheese will be bitter or over-sour in flavour. If the weather is cold, put the bowl of milk on a shelf in a store cupboard in a warm kitchen, or even in an airing cupboard. Leave the milk until it has 'jelled'. This can take up to 2 days (3-4 days is the maximum), but in warmer weather, or if a 'starter' has been used, it may jell overnight.

'Starters' hasten the jelling process. A cup of sour milk is the best starter, or use 1 tablespoon or more of yoghourt, depending on the quantity of milk.

Turn the 'jelly' into a piece of butter muslin and tie up to form a bag. Hang it to drip for 12 hours ; if the curd is rather soft, leave for a further 6-8 hours. The curd should be nicely firm but not too dry and crumbly.

Untie the muslin and scrape out the curd. Keep in a covered bowl until wanted, then either sieve or beat to remove any small lumps. Season with salt to taste.

French roasting (chicken)

Wipe the chicken inside with a damp cloth but do not wash the bird as this would hinder browning and do nothing to improve the flavour. Season inside as this will penetrate the flesh, whereas seasoning on the outside only would not, and the salt would draw out the juices and prevent browning. Put a good knob of butter and 3-4 sprigs of tarragon inside.

Truss the bird and rub well with butter. Place the chicken, breast side up, in a roasting tin with $\frac{1}{4}$ pint of chicken stock. Cover with buttered paper and roast for about 1 hour at 400°F or Mark 6.

After the first 15-20 minutes, when the flesh should be set but not coloured, baste and turn on one side. Baste and turn again after another 15-20 minutes and finish off with the breast side up again, removing the buttered paper for the last few minutes of roasting. The chicken should be well browned on all sides.

Garlic loaf

1 light loaf (eg. milk loaf)
1 clove of garlic
pinch of salt
2-4 oz butter (depending on size of loaf)

Method
Set oven at 400°F or Mark 6.

Cut loaf into slices to within ½ inch from bottom — take care not to go straight through.

Crush garlic with salt in a bowl, work in butter to give a creamy mixture. Spread butter on either side of each slice, leaving some butter over, and press loaf back into shape. Then spread top and side of loaf with remaining butter, tie securely with string, and put into pre-set oven. Heat through until crisp (about 15 minutes).

If only a slight hint of garlic is wanted, do not crush, but cut clove into quarters. Cream butter on its own then leave garlic lying in butter for 30 minutes. Remove garlic, then cream butter again to spread flavour through the mixture. The butter is then ready to spread on the loaf.

Grapefruit — preparation

To prepare grapefruit : halve, and using a small sharp knife, preferably with a curved and serrated blade, first cut out the core, then run the knife round the outside edge of the grapefruit, cutting between the flesh and the pith. Then slip knife either side of each membrane and lift out carefully without disturbing the segments of grapefruit. Carefully remove any pips.

Rice (boiled)

There are almost as many ways of cooking rice as there are cooks, so if you have your own well-tried method stick to it, but if you have problems, the following method is foolproof.

Allow 2 oz of washed rice per person.

Shower the rice into a large pan of boiling, salted water, at least 3 quarts for 8 oz, and add a slice of lemon for flavour. Stir with a fork to prevent sticking and boil steadily for about 12 minutes until tender. Rice very quickly overcooks so watch its cooking time carefully.

To stop rice cooking, tip it quickly into a colander and drain, or pour ½ cup of cold water into the pan and drain in a colander.

Then pour over a jug of hot water to wash away any remaining starch, making several holes through the rice (with the handle of a wooden spoon) to help it drain more quickly. Turn on to a large meat dish and leave in a warm place dry.

Turn rice from time to time with a fork.

For easy reheating, spoon rice into a well buttered, shallow fireproof dish which should be small enough for the rice to fill it amply. Place a sheet of well-buttered paper over the top. The rice can then be reheated and served in this dish. Allow 30 minutes in the oven at 350°F or Mark 4.

Stock (chicken)

This should ideally be made from the giblets (neck, gizzard, heart and feet, if available), but never the liver which imparts a bitter flavour. This is better kept for making pâté, or sautéd and used as a savoury. Dry fry the giblets with an onion, washed but not peeled, and cut in half. To dry fry, use a thick pan with a lid, with barely enough fat to cover the bottom. Allow the pan to get very hot before putting in the giblets and onion, cook on full heat until lightly coloured. Remove pan from heat before covering with 2 pints of cold water. Add a large pinch of salt, a few peppercorns and a bouquet garni (bayleaf, thyme, parsley) and simmer gently for 1-2 hours. Alternatively, make the stock when you cook the chicken by putting the giblets in the roasting tin around the chicken with the onion and herbs, and use the measured quantity of water.

Tomatoes (skinning and seeding)

Scald and skin tomatoes by placing them in a bowl, pouring boiling water over them, counting 12 before pouring off the hot water and replacing it with cold. The skin then comes off easily. Cut a slice from the top (not stalk end) of each tomato, reserve slices; hold tomato in hollow of your palm, flick out seeds with the handle of a teaspoon, using the bowl of the spoon to detach the core. So much the better if the spoon is worn and therefore slightly sharp.

Velouté sauce

¾ oz butter
1 rounded tablespoon flour
⅓ - ½ pint stock
2½ fl oz top of milk
salt and pepper
squeeze of lemon juice

For liaison (optional)
1 egg yolk (lightly beaten)
2 tablespoons cream

This sauce is made with a blond roux, at which point liquid is added. This is well-flavoured stock (made from veal, chicken or fish bones, according to dish with which sauce is being served), or liquid in which food was simmered or ·poached.

Velouté sauces are a base for others, such as caper, mustard, parsley, poulette or suprême.

Method
Melt butter in a saucepan, stir in flour and cook for about 5 seconds (blond roux). When roux is colour of pale straw, draw pan aside and cool slightly before pouring on stock.

Blend, return to heat and stir until thick. Add top of milk, season and bring to boil. Cook 4-5 minutes when sauce should be a syrupy consistency. If using a liaison, prepare by mixing egg yolk and cream together and then stir into sauce. Add lemon juice. Remove pan from heat.

Watchpoint Be careful not to let sauce boil after liaison has been added, otherwise the mixture will curdle.

Walnut bread & butter rolls

These are thin slices of brown bread and butter cut from a close-textured loaf, such as Hovis. (Putting the loaf, wrapped, in the ice compartment of the refrigerator for 30 minutes or so makes this job easier.)

Cut off the crust from the entire base of the loaf, butter and slice lengthways, ie. long slices from one end of the loaf to the other. Remove crusts and sprinkle with chopped walnuts and a little salt.

Starting from a short end, roll up two complete turns, then cut off, pressing the edge down firmly. Then continue until all the slice is used. Each slice should give 2-4 rolls, according to the size of the loaf.

Glossary

Blanch To whiten meats and remove strong tastes from vegetables by bringing to boil from cold water and draining before further cooking. Green vegetables should be put into boiling water and cooked for up to 1 minute.

Bouquet garni A bunch of herbs traditionally made up of 2-3 parsley stalks, a pinch of thyme and a bayleaf, tied with string if used in liquids which are later strained. Otherwise herbs are tied in a piece of muslin for easy removal before serving the dish.

Croûte Small round of bread, lightly toasted or fried, spread or piled up with a savoury mixture, also used as a garnish. The term is sometimes used to describe the cut shape of other foods, eg. aspic.

Deglaze To heat stock and / or wine together with flavoursome sediments left in roasting/frying pan so that gravy / sauce is formed. (Remove excess fat first.)

Dégorger To remove impurities and strong flavours before cooking by : 1 Soaking food, eg. uncooked ham, in cold water for specified length of time. 2 Sprinkling sliced vegetables, eg. cucumber, with salt, covering with heavy plate, leaving up to 1 hour, and pressing out excess liquid with a weighted plate.

Infuse To steep in liquid (not always boiling) in warm place to draw flavour into the liquid.

Julienne strip Strip of vegetable cut to about $\frac{1}{8}$ inch by $1\frac{1}{2}$-2 inches long.

Marinate To soak raw meat / game / fish in cooked or raw spiced liquid (marinade) of wine, oil, herbs and vegetables for hours / days before cooking.

Refresh To pour cold water over previously blanched and drained food.

Roux Fat and flour liaison (mixture). This is the basis of all flour sauces. The weight of fat should generally be slightly more than that of flour.

Index